CONQUER YOUR FEAR, SHARE YOUR FAITH

KIRK CAMERON
RAY COMFORT

CONQUER
YOUR FEAR
SHARE
YOUR
FAITH

Regal

From Gospel Light
Ventura, California, U.S.A.

Published by Regal
From Gospel Light
Ventura, California, U.S.A.
www.regalbooks.com
Printed in the U.S.A.

Library of Congress Cataloging-in-Publication Data
Comfort, Ray.
Conquer your fear, share your faith : evangelism made easy /
Ray Comfort and Kirk Cameron.
p. cm.
ISBN 978-0-8307-5154-9 (trade paper)
1. Witness bearing (Christianity) I. Cameron, Kirk, 1970- II. Title.
BV4520.C634 2009
269'.2—dc22
2009010298

2 3 4 5 6 7 8 9 10 / 15 14 13 12 11 10 09

Rights for publishing this book outside the U.S.A. or in non-English languages are
administered by Gospel Light Worldwide, an international not-for-profit ministry.
For additional information, please visit www.glww.org, email info@glww.org, or write to
Gospel Light Worldwide, 1957 Eastman Avenue, Ventura, CA 93003, U.S.A.

CONTENTS

INTRODUCTION

When I first heard the gospel message, I was 18 years old and still shooting episodes for *Growing Pains*. I was at the height of what the world defined as success, and yet I was dissatisfied. I had no concept of what a "soul" was, but I knew that if I had one, mine lacked something.

On one particular day, I agreed to go to church with a girl I was dating, and it just so happened that the man preaching that day was Chuck Swindoll. Mr. Swindoll talked about heaven and hell, about God's great mercy and love, and about how He created a way for people to be forgiven, purified and made new. Swindoll's words hit me deep inside. He wasn't one of those sweaty, purple-haired freaks I had seen on TV stealing money from gullible viewers. He didn't make big empty promises. Instead, he talked about how a person can find peace and a relationship with the creator of the universe. His words were sincere.

A month after my first visit to the church, I was sitting in my car when it occurred to me: *One day I will die.* As I pondered this thought, I felt completely overwhelmed. If God were up there in heaven, there was no reason for Him to let me in. My own pride, selfishness and sin had greatly offended Him. I had failed to give Him the honor and respect that He was due. I was sure that if I dropped dead on Van Nuys Boulevard at that very moment, God would have been perfectly justified to exclude me from paradise and give me what I deserved. That day, I made the decision to ask God to forgive my sins and change me into the person He wanted me to be.

However, it wasn't until years later after I had become a Christian that I really understood the depth to which I had violated God's Law. I was reading a book called *God Has a Wonderful Plan for Your Life: The Myth of the Modern Message* by Ray Comfort. The book was all about sharing the gospel with people the way Jesus did by using the Ten Commandments to help a sinner know why he needs a Savior. While this seems so obvious and basic to me now, no one had ever shared the gospel with me in that manner. So I decided to try out the approach on myself.

I opened my Bible to Exodus 20, went through each of the Commandments, and asked myself which ones I had broken. I quickly realized that I had broken all of them—even the ones like murder and adultery, because Jesus said that if you have hated and lusted, you are guilty of murder and adultery of the heart (see Matt. 5:21-28). For the first time, I seriously considered what it would be like to stand before an all-knowing and all-powerful God who saw me for what I truly was. It was an eye-opening experience, and over time I came to understand just how effective this approach could be when sharing the gospel with others.

I later watched a video of Ray open-air preaching in Central Park in New York City. He stood on a milk crate and made a spectacle of himself in the middle of a crowd. He was captivating. His words gripped my heart, and my eyes were glued to the video screen. Ray gave it to the people straight, kind of like a New Zealand version of the apostle Paul, about how they had violated God's Law and were under the penalty of eternal judgment. Then he told them about grace. He preached the cross, repentance and faith. He was straightforward, but he was compassionate. I could sense that he had a genuine concern for people and where they would spend eternity. Instead of people walking away from him, the crowd grew larger. I had never seen someone open-air preach so well, so passionately and so effectively. It was inspiring.

At first I had concerns about Ray's method of evangelism and wondered why few others were doing this. But as I read the New Testament, I realized that using the Ten Commandments to confront people with their sin was the method that Jesus and Paul also used. You can see a great example of this in Luke 18:18-22. In this passage, a certain ruler asks Jesus the following question: "Good Teacher, what shall I do to inherit eternal life?" Listen to Jesus' reply: "Why do you call Me good? No one is good but One, that is, God. You know the commandments: 'Do not commit adultery,' 'Do not murder,' 'Do not steal,' 'Do not bear false witness,' 'Honor your father and your mother.'"

I found when I was out witnessing with Ray that if I asked someone if he was a good person, he replied "yes" nearly every time. However, if I held up the mirror of the Ten Commandments, as Jesus did, and asked the person what he saw, he would realize very quickly that in the eyes of God, he was a guilty sinner. I thought this was amazing! For the first time, I didn't have to argue with someone about the truth of Romans 3:23 that "all have sinned and fall short of the glory of God." Once the person recognized his own sin, the step to seeing his need for a Savior wasn't such a great leap. This isn't a new principle; rather, this is the way of the Master!

In this book, and in the accompanying *Conquer Your Fear, Share Your Faith* four-session course, Ray and I will give you the basics you need to overcome your fear in sharing your faith with others. We will lay down some of the fundamentals for why each of us as Christians should share our faith and then demonstrate an effective way of sharing the gospel by using the Ten Commandments.

And we won't just tell you how—we'll also show you some practical examples of how we do it. We will look at some of the objections to this biblical method and how to deal with specific types of people: intellectuals, atheists, cult members and family members. Finally, we will take a look at a vital subject that Jesus spoke often about: "true and false conversion."

Thank you so much for picking up *Conquer Your Fear, Share Your Faith*. There is no higher calling than to share the gospel, and it is my prayer that as you read this book God will empower you to share the incredible good news of Christ with everyone you meet.

—Kirk Cameron

WHAT PETER FEARED

I stood in the lobby of a church and watched the TV monitor as the pastor told his congregation that he had stood on the side of the road the previous year holding a sign that said abortion was wrong. He then invited his congregation of 600 to join him this year and confirm their participation by raising a hand. Only 20 people raised their hands. I could sense his disappointment at their apathy. He then introduced me as the morning's guest speaker.

I told the congregation that I also felt passionate about the subject of abortion—and for a good reason. Many years ago, someone told me that a new Christian (we'll call her Fran) was about to take the life of her child through the procedure. I was horrified at the news, and when I found out she was due to have the procedure done within a couple of hours, I rushed to the hospital, praying all the way that God would give me the words to change her mind.

I ran up to the second floor and into her room. She was sitting up on the hospital bed and had already been administered her preoperational medication. *"Please* don't do this!" I pleaded. To my surprise, she just looked at me and smiled. Then she said,

"It's okay. I'm not going to have it. I just prayed, 'God, if you don't want me to have an abortion, make Ray Comfort come up and see me.'"

Two years later, I was at a church picnic and saw a beautiful little girl playing in the grass. It was Fran's child. Seeing her really hammered home the issue that we are dealing with when it comes to abortion.

I told the congregation that I would never, *ever*, vote for a person who advocated the murder of a child in the womb. I don't care how wonderful his or her fiscal policies were, because the blood of the innocent would be on his or her hands. I encouraged those in the congregation to follow the example of their faithful pastor. Later that afternoon, I heard that between 400 to 500 people turned out in support of the abortion protest. God bless them.

The Body of Christ in America is a sleeping giant that needs to be awakened. However, the answer to the issue of abortion isn't only to protest but also to preach. We are not to be salt only; we are also to be light in a spiritually dark nation. The fact that our nation kills 50 million of its citizens through abortion, with no qualms of conscience, needs more than a voice of protest. It needs the light of the gospel.

In this matter of abortion, we are no different from the crimes Nazi Germany committed during the Holocaust. We have given ourselves to the wickedest of sins, and that will eventually have terrible national consequences. We desperately need God's forgiveness, and we need a new heart that can only come through genuine conversion, which is salvation through Jesus Christ. Only the gospel can take a self-righteous, blaspheming, idolatrous, hypocritical, baby-killing nation and forgive it and make it brand new. That's the promise of the New Covenant:

Then I will sprinkle clean water on you, and you shall be clean; I will cleanse you from all your filthiness and from all your idols. I will give you a new heart and put a new spirit within you; I will take the heart of stone out of your flesh and give you a heart of flesh. I will put My Spirit within you and cause you to walk in My statutes, and you will keep My judgments and do them (Ezek. 36:25-27).

An Even Bigger Wake-up Call

The same kind of reluctance people feel about adding their voice to the issue of stopping abortion can be applied to speaking up to a world lost and dying for want of knowing why they need a Savior. Do you care about this nation? Do you care about this dying world? Then it's time for us to put legs to our prayers and do what we have been told to do, which is to be faithful laborers in the fields that are ready for harvest (see Matt. 9:37-38).

The Scriptures ask, "How shall they hear without a preacher?" (Rom. 10:14). The popular adage, "Preach the gospel; if necessary, use words," is like saying, "wash yourself; if necessary, use water." We *have* to use words if we want sinners to be saved. We live in desperate times, and we need to have clear and certain sounds to take us into the heat of battle. We have to overcome what I call "evangelophobia."

Two young men in security uniforms recently came to the door of our house. When they asked if I was interested in a security system, I said, "We already have a good system." When they asked what it was, I replied, "Celestial Security System. It's worked fine for us so far." Both men turned out to be Mormons, and after I explained that our security system was "the angel of the Lord [who] encamps all around those who fear Him, and delivers them" (Ps. 34:7), I asked what they thought happened after a person dies. There was no time to build a relationship, no living the Christian life in front of these young men, no waiting for the opportunity . . . and there was no offense. I used "words," and it worked. That's how humans best communicate, especially when it comes to the gospel. My question was simply a way to ask for their opinion, and they certainly had one.

When you enlisted in God's army to reach out to the lost, you can be sure that the enemy devised a strategy to keep you from the power you need to motivate you. So be ready for subtle thoughts of discouragement when you share your faith. Be ready for thoughts and words that have been designed to keep you from going anywhere and doing anything. They will often come from the least expected places. The enemy wants to cut off your source of fuel, because all your best intentions won't get you anywhere if you are not motivated.

We are going to look closely at where we get the fuel of motivation to share the gospel with others and how to keep it flowing into us. It comes at a high price, but it will be worth every drop. It is a high-octane fuel, and it has kept me moving since the moment of my conversion way back in April of 1972.

Where Is Jesus Sitting?

If you could rate how you are doing in your walk with God, how would you score yourself? If God were with you in your car, would you say that He's in the driver's seat? Is He in the passenger seat? In the back seat? Maybe in the trunk? While some people think it's okay to take God along as a passenger, He should be in total control, in every way. He should be steering your every move, because you should have surrendered control to Him at your moment of salvation (your conversion), and said, "Not my will, but Yours, be done." According to Scripture, that's our reasonable service:

> I beseech you therefore, brethren, by the mercies of God, that you present your bodies a living sacrifice, holy, acceptable to God, which is your reasonable service. And do not be conformed to this world, but be transformed by the renewing of your mind, that you may prove what is that good and acceptable and perfect will of God (Rom. 12:1-2).

That's the ideal, but in reality it hasn't happened with every Christian. How do I know that? Because so few Christians are involved in reaching out to the lost with the message that Jesus saves. They are heading in a different direction. They are busy doing other things. The other things may be legitimate, but if their house is on fire and people are sleeping in their beds, something isn't right if they begin dusting the living room. The situation dictates a radical change of priorities. They must forget the dusting, awaken those who are asleep and get them out of that burning house.

Every minute of every day, we must remember that people are being swallowed by death and are going to hell. Such a thought should consume the godly mind and drive each of us deeply into this dying world. That's the Great Commission (see Mark 16:15).

Where Are You in This Story?

Most of us are familiar with what happened just before Jesus went to the cross:

> Coming out, He went to the Mount of Olives, as He was accustomed, and His disciples also followed Him. When

He came to the place, He said to them, "Pray that you may not enter into temptation." And He was withdrawn from them about a stone's throw, and He knelt down and prayed, saying, "Father, if it is Your will, take this cup away from Me; nevertheless not My will, but Yours, be done" (Luke 22:39-42).

We know the disciples didn't pray; they went to sleep. Sleep is a refuge for the depressed, and they were depressed by what they saw—a distressed Jesus of Nazareth. Think of it. This was the one who controlled the storms they had feared would drown them. This was the one who raised the dead and turned water into wine. This was the one who was in total control. But something was wrong.

Imagine seeing Jesus just after He had been in agony, with His sweat coming out of His pores like great drops of blood falling to the ground. Then Judas arrived with a mob, including soldiers, to arrest Jesus. Impetuous Peter jumped to Jesus' defense, took a sword and lopped off the ear of the servant of the high priest, and then the disciples scattered like frightened sheep without a shepherd. Jesus was arrested and taken to the house of Caiaphas, the high priest. We are told, "But Peter followed at a distance" (Luke 22:54), and then he sat down by a fire with some men and warmed himself. A servant girl and others questioned him as to whether he was a disciple of Jesus, but he adamantly denied it—three times. It took a rooster to waken him to what he was doing, and he went out and wept bitterly.

Two Big Mistakes

Peter made two very big mistakes on that cold and dark night. His first mistake was that instead of praying to avoid temptation (as

Jesus had told him to do), he slept. That's easy to do, especially when you are depressed. Sleep is a pleasant refuge from life's storms. But the restful break from reality came at a terrible cost. If Peter had been praying, he may have had his own Gethsemane experience. Perhaps Peter would have said, "I'm scared, Father. I'm depressed. I am horrified at what seems to be happening. I feel like running away from this, but I'm Yours. I will stay with Jesus no matter what. This is not about what I want, but about what You want." Instead, he slept. His spirit was willing, but his flesh was weak.

His second mistake was that he followed Jesus at a distance. Jesus had said to him, "Follow Me, and I will make you to fishers of men" (Matt. 4:19), and he had followed Jesus and in His shadow for more than three years, but this night we are told that he followed Jesus "at a distance." Consequently, he was able to sit in the midst of the ungodly for one whole hour without any thought for their eternal wellbeing. When the opportunity arose—when someone asked him if he was a follower of Jesus—he avoided the truth like the plague. Fear paralyzed him into silence.

At face value, this incident makes no sense. Peter risked his life to defend Jesus in the Garden of Gethsemane. He said that he would die with Jesus. He had courageously ignored his fears and stepped out of a boat to walk on water just to be with Jesus. So why was he suddenly afraid to say that he was a follower of Jesus? I don't think it was because Peter was ashamed of Jesus of Nazareth. I think it was something greater. We know from Scripture that Peter was impetuous. He didn't think too deeply.

Impetuosity has its pros and cons. I know that from experience. My own life is full of excitement because I am a risk taker. I tend to step out of the boat onto the water. I don't think too much about failure, but fail I often do. My wife, Sue, is horrified if I see a fly in our kitchen, because I tend to go for it without any concern for the consequences. I can't help it. I will grab anything (within reason) and chase that fly down until it leaves this life. That means that anything in the way gets knocked over in the process.

Peter was like that when he defied logic and walked on the surface of the sea. Who in the entire human race can say they have done that? Only impetuous Peter. And he wasn't thinking too deeply when he cut off the ear of the high priest's servant in the Garden of Gethsemane. There was a "fly" heading for Jesus, so Peter swatted it.

As he sat by the fire, however, and warmed his chilly hands, he had time to think. Jesus had been arrested. Peter knew that the Jews wanted Him dead. They had tried to kill Jesus before, and this time they had Him. We know from Scripture that Peter was within viewing distance from Jesus, because when Jesus looked at Peter after the rooster crowed, Peter realized what he had done. So Peter may have witnessed the cruel mockery and the terrible beating Jesus endured. He probably knew what was going to happen. There was no justice in Rome. They were the occupation, and Jews were nothing but scum to them. Crucifixion was common—they even crucified thieves!

What Peter Feared

I may be wrong, but it seems to me that the Roman cross was what Peter feared. He feared crucifixion. Crosses were all over Jerusalem, stained with the blood of criminals who had violated Roman law, and the bodies were left hanging for all to see. This was no mere lethal injection. It was cruel but usual punishment. The Romans had raised the crossbar of human suffering to a

COURAGE

One of the most necessary virtues of a firefighter is courage. You don't want him turning around and running at the first sign of danger. He is willing to suffer pain to do his duty. That takes a special person.

We have the ultimate example of courage in Jesus of Nazareth, who went to the unspeakable pain of the cross to save us from the agony of hell.

There is a story of a farmer who walked through his farm after a fire had burned everything to the ground. He looked at a dead and smoldering chicken for a moment, and then pushed it with his foot. To his amazement, he found that beneath its wings were live chicks. The mother had lovingly spread her wings and sheltered them from the fire. Such is the love of God for us. In Christ, God spread the wings of His love to save us from the consuming fire of His eternal justice.

Jesus likened the love of God to a hen covering her chicks. He said, "O Jerusalem, Jerusalem, the one who kills the prophets and stones those who are sent to her! How often I wanted to gather your children together, as a hen gathers her brood under her wings, but you were not willing!" (Luke 13:34).

He is our example. If God so loved us, we must love those who are in danger of the vengeance of eternal fire. May God give us a compassion that will swallow our natural fears and drive us to pull others from the fire, hating even the garment that is singed by the flesh.

—Kirk Cameron

terrifying level. The cross was intended to cause fear. It was a grisly public display—a freeway billboard designed to deter the busy traffic of crime.

So, more than likely, Peter was very familiar with the cross. He had no doubt seen soldiers dutifully hold down unwilling and grasping hands and nailing them to the wooden beam. He had probably seen men writhe as barbed Roman steel penetrated their tender flesh. He had been a silent witness as hardened men became screaming animals, and he was horrified by the stark reality of what was happening. Perhaps he had heard them plead for death to rescue them. One look into their eyes was enough to terrorize the most callous of human hearts.

No, I don't think it was the servant girl that Peter feared. I think it was the terrifying threat of the Roman torture stake.

I don't blame Peter for being afraid. I cringe when I think of the unspeakable cruelty of the cross. I think about how I feel when I have a splinter in my hand and Sue tries to dig it out with a needle. I have to turn my head, because tears from the pain fill my eyes. No doubt about it—I'm the chief of wimps. I preach a lot in the open air, and one of my favorite verses is that if we are persecuted in one city, Jesus said to flee to the next. That sounds good to me. I'm not waiting around to be stoned to death. In fact, I have often said that one of the first rules of open-air preaching is to check that there are no stones lying around.

Many years ago, I read about a Moslem woman who was stoned to death for adultery. It took 15 minutes for the woman to die. Fifteen long minutes. So, if people wanted to kill me for my faith, I wouldn't hesitate to follow Paul's example to be lowered over a wall in a basket to escape their clutches. I don't mind pain as long as it doesn't hurt.

What We Fear

So, I truly empathize with Peter's fear of the cross. Perhaps you are like me. Maybe you don't like pain either. Maybe you are a little impetuous, and you would quickly take up the sword of the Word of God to defend Jesus. But perhaps you are more like Peter than you realize. Let's ask a few probing questions. It's a little chilly, so come closer to the fire so you can warm your hands. Let's see how cold they are.

When did you last reach out a hand to the lost? When did you last share the bloodied cross? When did you last preach Christ crucified for the sin of the world? I'm not asking if you can argue with an evolutionist or mop the floor with an atheist. I'm not asking about your exegesis, your hermeneutics or your presuppositional apologetics. I'm not asking about your good works or your worship. I'm asking if you, like Paul, have determined not to know anything among the ungodly except Jesus Christ and Him crucified (see 1 Cor. 2:2). Or are you afraid of what Scripture calls the "offense of the cross"? Like Peter, you dread the cross because of the personal pain it will bring. What do I mean by that?

I have found that I can have a certain respect from listeners if I preach or witness about evolution, the principles of a godly marriage, the need for godly legislation in politics and certain other subjects. But when I preach the cross and talk about sin—when I open up the Ten Commandments and speak of righteousness and judgment—it brings out a painful disdain from my listeners.

The famous clergyman John Newton (1725-1807) spoke about the world's reaction to the gospel. In reference to Acts 17:18 ("What does this babbler want to say?"), Newton said:

> The apostles were accounted babblers. . . . We are no better than the apostles; nor have we reason to expect much better treatment, so far as we walk in their steps. On the other hand, there is a sober decent way of speaking of God, and goodness, and benevolence, and sobriety, which the world will bear well enough. . . . But if we preach Him as the only foundation, lay open the horrid evils of the human heart, tell our hearers that they are dead in trespasses and sins, and have no better ground of hope in themselves than the vilest malefactors . . . if we tell the virtuous and decent, as well as the profligate, that unless they are born again, and made partakers of living faith, and count all

things loss for the excellency of the knowledge of Christ, they cannot be saved; this is the world cannot bear. We shall be called knaves or fools, uncharitable bigots, and twenty hard names. If you have met with nothing like this, I wish it may lead you to suspect whether you have yet received the right key to the doctrines of Christ; for, depend upon it, the offense of the cross is not ceased.[1]

The cross carries a reproach. It stirs up hatred from a sin-loving, God-hating world. And so, my intellectual dignity wants to avoid the cross. So what's the answer to this dilemma? What is the fuel that motivates us to ignore our fears? We will look at the specifics of this in the next chapter.

IRKSOME WORDS THAT CONVICT

The cross has a certain reproach about it, because it brings with it some heavy baggage that our weak flesh would rather not carry. Our flesh wants to avoid the pain of the cross. Preaching the cross means that we have to tell the world about sin and about our responsibility toward God for our thoughts, words and deeds. Preaching the cross means that we have to speak of God's anger against humanity and of the reality of a terrible place called hell. These are not pleasant subjects. In fact, they are extremely irksome and even painful to speak about. So it's understandable to want to skirt around the cross and what it means and speak of more pleasant things that bring smiles rather than frowns.

My wife and I have a bird feeder by a window in our living room where I do most of my writing. Every day I watch birds feeding, fluttering, fighting and then flying off. But, as a Christian, I can't help but think more deeply about what I witness every day. Each one of these little creatures is an amazingly made independent flying machine. I have read the biography of the Wright brothers and was fascinated by the fact that they continually studied principles of flight that they saw in birds before they constructed their own flying machine. We now have the miracle of flight because the Wright brothers copied God's handiwork. They watched as birds twisted their wings in flight, and observed how they used their tail as a rudder. If God hadn't given the Wright brothers and others clues through His creation, we would probably still be grounded today.

I watch these little birds land in a tiny space with absolute precision, flutter their amazingly made wings and move their heads with incredibly delicate movements. Each one has its own personality and a mind to feed on what will benefit it. It has a memory of where the food is and instinctively mixes with birds of its own kind, but its tiny eyes are peeled for cats. One cat, or the movement of my hand, and a dozen of them will leave in an instant. They don't panic at the first sign of danger and fly into each other, but in a split second they fly away in amazing unison. It's not as if one of them sounds an alarm and they leave. It's an instantaneous exit.

Each bird has a tiny brain, muscles that move the tail and twist the wings, a sense of thirst, a sense of hunger and an instinct to build a home, start a family and search for food by day and snooze at night. They have a brain that coordinates tiny feet, wings, a stomach, digestive juices, lungs that pull in air, kidneys, bowels, a liver, blood and a pumping heart that sends it and oxygen through the tiny brain that keeps each little bird alive and kicking.

As Christians, we often talk about such wonders of creation that reveal the genius of our wonderful Creator. However, to reach a godless world with the gospel, we can't confine ourselves to preaching the pleasantries of intelligent design. We must preach the intelligent *Designer*. We are to preach the *person* of Jesus Christ. Scripture tells us that He was the one (before His incarnation) who created all things. There wasn't a thing that was made that wasn't made by Him (see John 1:3-14). Listen to the apostle Paul tell us the content of his preaching: "For we preach not ourselves, but Christ Jesus the Lord" (2 Cor. 4:5). He also says, "But we preach Christ crucified" (1 Cor. 1:23). Why does he do this? He tells us why in 1 Corinthians 2:1-5:

> And I, brethren, when I came to you, did not come with excellence of speech or of wisdom declaring to you the testimony of God. For I determined not to know anything among you except Jesus Christ and Him crucified. I was with you in weakness, in fear, and in much trembling. And my speech and my preaching were not with persuasive words of human wisdom, but in demonstration of the Spirit and of power, that your faith should not be in the wisdom of men but in the power of God.

Paul is talking about the gospel—the *person* of Jesus Christ and Him crucified. The gospel message has the power of God to bring about salvation. Without an understanding of the cross, there can be no salvation. You may get a "decision" from a sinner, but if that person doesn't put his or trust in the living person of Jesus Christ, he or she isn't saved.

If we simply use apologetics to bring people to a decision for Christ, we may, like a zealous Peter, end up cutting off ears. Our churches are filled with people who show no signs that they have been regenerated by the Holy Spirit. They believe in God and they believe in Jesus, but they don't demonstrate the things that accompany salvation. They have made a decision based on man's wisdom and not because of a demonstration of the Spirit and His power. Their faith stands on the wisdom of men, not in the power of God. These people are almost unreachable. They are inoculated against the true gospel because they think they are saved when it's apparent they are not.

I'm not advising you to avoid apologetics. In fact, I published a Bible that is filled with apologetic arguments.[1] Rather, the discourse of apologetics should be the means to an end, with that end being the cross. For without the cross, sinners cannot be saved. J. C. Ryle said:

> Let others, if they will, preach the Law and morality. Let others hold forth the terrors of hell and the joys of heaven. Let others drench their congregations with teachings about the sacraments and the church. Give me the cross of Christ. This is the only lever which has ever turned the world upside down hitherto, and made men forsake their sins.[2]

If you and I are avoiding the cross, it may be that we have missed our Gethsemane experience. We have never presented our bodies as a living sacrifice and prayed, "Not my will, but Yours, be done." And so we follow Jesus at a distance. Consequently, we live in the midst of the ungodly without any real concern for their eternal welfare, as evidenced by our avoidance of the cross.

Running the Streets Mad

An atheist once wrote to me and said, "If you believed one bit that thousands every day were falling into an eternal and unchangeable fate, you should be running the streets mad with rage at their blindness. That's equivalent to standing on a street corner and watching every person that passes you walk blindly, directly into the path of a bus and die, yet you stand idly by and do nothing."

Listen to his words: "If you believed one bit that thousands every day were falling into an eternal and unchangeable fate, *you should be running the streets mad with rage at their blindness.*" I wrote back and said, "That's what I do!" I am horrified that any person could end up in hell. Whenever I hit my thumb with a hammer or feel the pain of the dentist's drill hitting a nerve, I think of the fate of those who die in their sins. These aren't pleasant thoughts, but they are thoughts we must entertain if we are going to have a concern for the lost. Charles Spurgeon said:

> If sinners will be damned, at least let them leap to hell over our bodies. And if they will perish, let them perish with our arms about their knees, imploring them to stay. If hell must be filled, at least let it be filled in the teeth of our exertions, and let not one go there unwarned and unprayed for.[3]

Is that the case in contemporary America? Do we see preachers pleading with the lost in their churches? Do we see the average Christian deeply concerned for the salvation of the unsaved? Listen to the words of the late Bill Bright, the founder of Campus Crusade for Christ:

> Here in the United States, one-third of all adults identify themselves as born-again, evangelical Christians. . . . But we have a serious problem. These facts are not reflected in the life of our nation. According to our surveys . . . a bare two percent regularly share their faith in Christ. Obviously something is tragically wrong.[4]

Think of it: While the world is on its way to hell, how much of the contemporary Church is reaching out to them with the gospel? A mere two percent. What a terrible indictment on the wickedness of our nature—that we would have to be *told* to take the words of everlasting life to a dying world. What does it say about the character of a doctor who has a cure in his hand and yet needs to be *told* to give it to a dying patient? You shouldn't be able to hold him back!

"Excuse me, doctor, but why are you just standing there instead of helping that patient?"

"Because I don't know what to say."

"What do you mean, you don't know what to say? That's ridiculous. Have you ever given it some thought? You are supposed to be a doctor. Tell him he's deathly sick and that you have a cure."

"What if he asks a question I can't answer?"

"Just say, 'I don't know how to answer that question, but I will try to find the answer and get back to you.'"

"What if he rejects me?"

"That's his problem, not yours. All you are morally obligated to do is tell him about the cure to his terminal disease."

"But I'm not gifted to speak to him."

"Why don't you be honest? You couldn't care less about this dying patient. You are just looking for excuses. Shame on you. You don't deserve to be called a doctor."

What is wrong with us? We are supposed to have the love of God in our hearts, but our hearts are like stone. Every minute of every day people are dying and going to hell, yet we search for excuses not to talk with them. We should want to shout the gospel from the housetops.

Personalize Your World

I recently read a biography of Abraham Lincoln by David Colins. It was written in Lincoln's own words, based on historical records. As I turned each page, I wondered how the author would handle his assassination, because Lincoln obviously didn't say anything after he was shot in the head. Subconsciously I was thinking, *What is the author going to say? "And there I was, sitting in Ford's Theatre, watching a play, when someone shot me in the head, and I died"*? That wouldn't make any sense.

In the book, Lincoln spoke of the grief of the Civil War, how good it was to have peace back in the country, and how he went to a play with his wife. It was a comedy, so he spoke about how it was good to hear people laugh again. He said, "To be with Mary . . . to think of the years ahead. Please, God, never let people forget the joy of love, the pleasure of laughter, and the beauty of peace." Then there was simply a bold headline that read: "WASH-INGTON, D.C.—President Abraham Lincoln was shot at Ford's Theatre shortly after ten o'clock last evening. At 7:22 this morning, April 15, 1865, he died."[5]

As I read those words, tears ran down my cheeks. I couldn't believe my reaction. From the moment I picked up the book I knew it was coming, so why was I crying like a child? The reason is because throughout the book, I got to *know* Abraham Lincoln—not just as some a cold historical figure, but as a man with fears and pains.

I grieved when his beloved sister suddenly died in her youth. I mourned with him at the loss of two of his children through terrible sickness. I felt for him when he questioned why God would give him and his beloved wife such wonderful children and then let death seize them. The book *personalized* Lincoln to a point in which, when the assassination came, I personally felt the pain of his untimely death.

Did you know that every 24 hours, 150,000 people die? That's a lot of people—150,000—every day. That's almost 2 Superbowls full. But because it's just a cold statistic, it can wash over us like water on a dead duck's back. If we are going to have a passion for the unsaved, we have to *personalize* them to the point in which their lostness brings more than a tear to the eye. We have to see that those 150,000 people who are being swallowed by death every day are beloved moms and dads, sons and daughters, brothers and sisters—people with the same fears and pains that visit us. That is what is known as empathy, a virtue of compassion that causes us to feel the pain of another.

A Needed Outlet

Nothing lives in the Dead Sea. It is some of the saltiest water on earth, and it gets saltier with increasing depth. It's almost six times as salty as the ocean. It's called the "dead" sea because it is completely landlocked and has no outlet. It is continually fed from the rivers and streams coming down off the mountains that surround it, but no rivers drain out of the Dead Sea.

How the modern Church is like the Dead Sea! It is rich with teaching, but it has no outlet. It doesn't reach out to the lost. I don't think there have ever been a people in Church history so rich in knowledge as people are today. Years ago, it was prestigious to own the complete Matthew Henry commentaries or all of Spurgeon's sermons. It meant that the owner could read through them and become rich in knowledge. Nowadays, we can have instant Spurgeon or any other preacher or commentator through the Internet. It's faster than a drive-through. In seconds, we can find out what almost any preacher has said about almost any subject. Consequently, we have become richer in knowledge than any other generation. But, in truth, the contemporary Church is wretched, poor, blind, miserable and naked. We have so much, and yet we have done so little to reach out to the lost.

One-third of all adults in the United States identify themselves as born-again, evangelical Christians. That's more than 100 million people.[6] They must be everywhere in our society. I must pass them on the sidewalks, in the mall, in my car, in the store. Yet I have been on more than 2,000 flights (many in the United States) and *never once* has the person sitting next to me tried to witness to me. So where are the 100 million people who have the love of Christ in them? Where does one find concern for the lost?

A great preacher once said, "We must be ashamed at the mere suspicion of unconcern." We don't have a mere suspicion—our inaction as a Church shows that we are *completely* unconcerned.

A Changed Life

A young man wrote to us recently about the change that had occurred in his life after he accepted Christ. He said that he had been cutting himself, but that he had come to a point of realizing that he needed a Savior and had repented of his sins and put his faith in Jesus. This is what he said in his email:

> As I sat there, it was like all my pain dripped off, washed away forever in Christ's blood. I felt so relieved that I can't even describe it. Then I looked at my arms, and my scars made me sick. Before, they were a part of me. Now, they feel sinful. . . . I am amazed that I once used pain to make me feel alive. . . . If you could, please tell others that there

are guys like me out there that just need to hear this message of salvation. I have friends that are in the same position I was, and I'm going to tell them as soon as I can.

The fruit of a genuine conversion is an inability to sit with cold hands among the ungodly without concern that they are going to be damned in hell. The problem is that many people aren't *genuinely* converted. They have never heard the true gospel, and so they have never really seen Jesus Christ evidently set forth and crucified. They haven't been brought to the foot of His blood-stained cross. They were brought to a "decision" when they should have been brought to a place of repentance because they had offended a holy God who sees lust as adultery and hatred as murder. They were never shown their sin by hearing the spiritual nature of the moral Law (the Ten Commandments) in the light of New Testament revelation.

Just Get the Words Out

I was once having a blood test. When the nurse came in to prepare the needle, I said to her, "What's your name?"

"Polly."

"Polly, what do you think happens after someone dies? Do you think there is a heaven?"

"I don't know."

"Do you think that there is a hell?"

"I don't know."

"If there were a heaven, do you think you are good enough to go there? Are you a good person?"

"Yes, I am."

She seemed very open, so I said, "There's one way to find out.

Simply look at the Ten Commandments for two minutes."

She said, "Oh, I used to do that all the time!" (She thought I was referring to the movie!)

This incident reminded me of another time I was in an elevator with a businessman. I had to be quick, because he was only going down a couple of floors, so in this case I used a special resource to help start the conversation.[7] I handed him a penny with the Ten Commandments imprinted on it. I said, "Did you get one of these?" As he looked at it and noticed the writing, I said, "It's a penny with the Ten Commandments on it. How many commandments have you kept?" He looked at the penny again and said, "It's the first one I've been given," and walked out of the elevator.

These are just a couple of examples of people you and I meet every day of our lives. Neither person I spoke with had a clue about the life-giving message of salvation in Jesus Christ. Even though I didn't lead these people to a decision for Christ, my words and actions planted a seed that may get watered and harvested at a later time. What if I hadn't spoken as I did? The nurse would have continued to think that God's Ten Commandments was a movie. And the man in the elevator might have left this life never having thought much about why every man, woman and child needs a Savior.

Stay with me, because I next want to tell you something interesting about my beloved chickens. Most of us have something in common with them . . .

LOOSENING
THE STRING OF
THE TONGUE

Sue and I have a chicken coop. There is something wonderful about picking fresh eggs out of a nest every day. And that's why we have chickens—to give us fresh eggs. So, to remind the "ladies" as to why they exist, I named them and put their names on the wall of their coop. Their names are: Original, Finger-lickin', Roasted, Tender and Crispy (I even put a picture of Colonel Sanders beside their names). I often ask them, "What will it be for dinner tonight—eggs . . . or chicken?" They have plenty of clean straw, food and fresh water. I like to think of my chicken coop as the chickens' "happiest place on earth."

I've learned a lot from these ladies. They are extremely bold—especially when they think I have some food in my hand. They will jump up and peck my wedding ring or my hand looking for food. But if my hand comes down toward them as though I am about to pick them up, they shake. They squat and physically tremble.

How like chickens we are! We are bold in many areas, especially when it comes to getting "stuff" from God. We peck at Bible verses that shine and seem to have value for us. How many of us have underlined the verse, "Delight yourself also in the LORD, and He shall give you the desires of your heart" (Ps. 37:4)? But when His hand comes upon us to do His will—to preach and witness about the blood of the cross to a God-hating world, we cringe like frightened chickens.

Let me ask you a question: Could you get up on a soapbox and preach the gospel to strangers? Is that scary for you? I have had friends say that preaching the gospel for the first time was about as frightening as the first time they tried skydiving. Perhaps you can identify with that. But it makes no sense. Think about it: If something goes wrong when you are preaching and you have to jump off the box, you fall toward the earth and hit the ground at about 2 MPH. Big deal. However, if something goes wrong when you are skydiving, you fall to the earth and hit the ground at 120 MPH. Your life is over. Which is truly more frightening: to preach the gospel on the street corner or to jump out of a plane and wonder if your parachute will open?

I have a confession to make: I have an agenda. I want to see the contemporary Church shake off the chickens and be bold as lions. I want to see the modern Church act like the Church in the book of Acts. I want to see the Body of Christ act as though it has found everlasting life. I want to see it boldly going "into all the world," preaching the "gospel to every creature."

Notice the wording of the Great Commission in Matthew 28:19-20. It says that we are to go *into* the world. This is because the world isn't going to come to us. Those in the world love the darkness and hate the light. *Neither will they come to the light lest their deeds are exposed* (see John 3:19-20). So we have to take the gospel to them.

Before Jesus Comes Again

When it comes to hurricanes, tornadoes, floods and even the economy, secular news often sounds as if it has gone Christian. Newscasters talk about "acts of God" and things happening in "biblical proportions." They are right to do so. The frequency of occurrence of these things is unprecedented in human history.

Every time I see an act of lawlessness, a dead church system, a nation rising against another nation, people loving pleasure and ignoring God, an increase in immorality, turmoil in the Middle East, a collapse of a financial system and even the rise of atheism (rebellion against God), I check off another sign of the end of the age and the issuing in of the literal kingdom of God.

Of all times in history, this isn't a time for Christians to sit back and do nothing. One of the signs that Jesus spoke of regarding the end times was the preaching of the gospel. Are you doing that? Are you reaching out to those deceived by sin? Do you care that in a moment of time they can be swallowed by death? Then *do something*. Go somewhere, find someone and say something. Learn to take people through the Ten Commandments to show them why they need a Savior.

Does such a thought make you fearful? You are not alone. Fear is the venom of the enemy. It is meant to paralyze you. Look at this comment from a brother who decided to reach out to the lost:

> On the season two *The Way of the Master* DVD, "How to Get on Fire for God," you made mention that even after all these years you can still feel an anxiousness in your stomach prior to going out. The attacks I've felt have been fierce! Even after saying I would go, on the second trip, I was feeling so attacked that my wife told me I could always

ncel—just tell them I wasn't feeling well.
n the desk and could barely move. My
ning. All the fears surfaced—you don't
...ough, you'll sound stupid, it's your pride working, you'll lead someone down the wrong path, you'll chase
them away, and on and on. Only by the power of the Holy
Spirit, who reminded me that even after all these years you,
Ray, still feel those attacks, helped me to lift my head off
that desk, grab my keys and run out the door! I could go
on with how I talked to three different gentlemen in Spanish, which I haven't used in years. "Rusty" would be an understatement! Still, God is faithful, and even while my
mind was searching for the words, my mouth was already
saying them. I haven't even practiced the Ten Commandments in Spanish, much less the gospel.

Don't listen to your fears; listen to your faith. Fear whispers
that you can't. Faith says that you can, because faith brings God
into the equation. Faith runs toward Goliath.

Why are we so fearful when it comes to public preaching? The
answer is evident: We are fearful of looking foolish—of our minds
going blank and being unable to speak. We're fearful of looking
foolish because we can't answer a question, and we don't want to
humiliate ourselves. In other words, we want our listener's ap-
proval. So our fear will be in direct proportion to our pride. A
proud person is concerned about how he or she will look to others. But love and concern for the welfare of our hearers should
cause us to quickly say, "I don't care about myself. I care about
the eternal fate of these people. They are going to hell, and I must
warn them!"

Have No Regrets

So, what are your personal fears about sharing the gospel? I hope you have at least one, because that means you are serious about reaching the unsaved. Is it that your words will dry up and you'll make a fool of yourself? If it is, I have a backup parachute for you. Keep a New Testament in your hand, and if your mind goes blank, open it to John 3:16, read it, say "thank you," and then jump off the box.

When I think of unwise decisions that lead to regret, I usually think of cigarette smokers and skydivers. What must a person be thinking who is slowly suffocating to death because he or she smoked cigarettes? How crazy is it to breathe smoke into your lungs? It's like poking your eye every day with a needle and then wondering why you are going blind. Every instinct should say that smoking is insane.

What about someone who suddenly realizes that his or her parachute is twisted and that he or she is plummeting toward the ground at 120 MPH? I wonder what that person's last thoughts are. That his or her body will be smashed to pieces on impact? That he or she will never see his or her loved ones again? Is that person thinking, *Why did I choose to do this when every instinct within me screamed not to do it?* (By the way, if you can't seem to shake the insanity of wanting to skydive or do some other kind of risky behavior because you want to experience the adrenaline rush, try open-air preaching instead. Someone may find everlasting life because you opened your mouth rather than your parachute.)

If some life decisions, like smoking and skydiving, seem unwise, how much more will we regret the decision to keep quiet about the gospel when Judgment Day comes? People often quote the famous verse, "Remember now your Creator in the days of your youth" (Eccles. 12:1), and direct it toward the unsaved when they should also apply it to themselves.

If God allows you to grow old, the day will come when your spirit is willing but your flesh is weak. You may find yourself sitting in a chair with a blanket over you to keep you warm. Your voice trembles, your hands tremble, and your mind can't articulate a clear gospel presentation. You find that *any* communication is difficult. You think of the energy of your youth and how quick on your feet mentally you were in those days. You whisper to yourself, *Oh, how I wasted my youth on vanities! I should have served God when I was able to think and move and speak.*

Unleash Your Tongue

In Mark 7:35, a deaf man who had an impediment in his speech was brought to Jesus. Jesus put His fingers onto the man's ears and said, "Be opened," and we are told, "the string of his tongue was loosed." Suddenly, he could speak! Jesus told those who saw the incident to keep it under their hats. They couldn't. They shouted what they had seen and heard from the housetops.

Perhaps God has been touching your ears through this book to the end that your tongue will be loosed to share the gospel. Is that what you want? I hope so. I hope that you have come to the point of saying that if someone told you not to preach Christ crucified, you would say, "I cannot but speak that which I have seen and heard!"

Are you beginning to see the need of adding your voice to those who share the gospel? If you're still not convinced, and if I can't appeal to your compassion for the lost, maybe I can appeal to your selfishness to at least get you started. I can hear someone saying, "But that's not a good motive to be preaching!" True. It's not a good motive. But read what the apostle Paul said about motives for preaching the gospel:

> Some indeed preach Christ even from envy and strife, and some also from goodwill: The former preach Christ from selfish ambition, not sincerely, supposing to add affliction to my chains; but the latter out of love, knowing that I am appointed for the defense of the gospel. What then? Only that in every way, whether in pretense or in truth, Christ is preached; and in this I rejoice, yes, and will rejoice (Phil. 1:15-18).

Even when someone preached Christ from a *bad* motive, Paul rejoiced. Why? Because it doesn't really matter *why* a person reaches out to the lost as long as he or she *does* it. Imperfect motives for preaching the gospel still get people to hear those life-saving words.

But is there such a thing as a "perfect" motive? That's something we will look at in the next chapter.

THE SOURCE OF OUR MUCH-NEEDED POWER

Do you pray often? I hope you do, because it is in secret prayer that we find the source of our much-needed power.

I pray best at night because I am easily distracted by the goings-on of the day. For years I have gone to bed early, wakened around midnight most nights each week, and risen for prayer. I always grab a blanket (yes, it is a "security" blanket) to wrap around me, and then I kneel on the floor in the dark. The blanket and the darkness not only give me a sense of security but also a sense of intimacy with God. I have a pen and paper beside me. I begin with soul searching.

We all know that it's wise to keep a check on our flesh for skin cancer. What may look small on the surface may be a network of death beneath the skin. The same applies spiritually. One harsh word or thought may be the sign of something deeper that has death written all over it. One lust-filled glance may be quickly forgotten during the business of the day, but prayer tends to bring it to mind. We often call this having a "quiet time" with the Lord.

And that's what it should be, for it's in the quiet that we can hear the voice of our conscience under the influence of the Holy Spirit.

I recently received the following email from a woman who was rejoicing in her salvation. She had been brought to the cross's saving power through having a quiet time of prayer:

> I heard about *The Way of the Master*, and by reading the book and just trying to find out everything I could, I became saved. It happened on about the third day after I started having a quiet time. I looked up and realized how awful I had been and how good God is, and how intently He had been pursuing me even though I was awful and a persistent runner. I was what you guys would call a "backslider"; I have gone to church my entire life and had been fed the "modern gospel" and, yes, I had asked Jesus into my heart many times before.
>
> That was another thing I never understood: I had tried and tried to ask Jesus into my heart, and it angered me because I never felt Him there. I was so mad at God because I was praying and I didn't feel anything, and I didn't understand. I wanted God to make me feel better, but He didn't. Anyway, I did bad things throughout my adolescence, and then I would feel guilty about them, but I still thought I was saved, because people always said that you know you are saved when you do something you shouldn't and you feel guilty about it. . . .
>
> Anyway, I am saved now. Thank God! Since I have known about *The Way of the Master*, I have seen how the modern gospel—"Hell's Best Kept Secret"—is killing people. It infuriates me. I could have been one of those people.

All of those years I had been taught a certain way, and I should have seen the signs of how it was wrong, but I didn't know any different. I recently had brain surgery, and it is scary to think how close I came to dying without going to heaven. That is really scary and very upsetting.

The preachers I used to look at and think, *Wow, they are refreshing, I like listening to them,* I now look at with frustration and see how they are basically ignoring Jesus' words. I used to get sick when I listened to a preacher give a sermon about Judgment Day and God's wrath, but now I am so proud to hear those preachers preach that, because they truly care more about the people in the church than they do about themselves. It is so nice to have my eyes opened. Thank God, in time!

Personal Sin Revealed

Spending time with the Lord is a precious time of getting close to Him. So when I have my quiet time, I pray that God would search me and know my heart, try me and know my thoughts, and see if there is any wicked way in me (see Ps. 139:23-24). I'm not too concerned with pride. I can usually detect that in myself when it raises its big, ugly head. I am more concerned with something deeper—the cancer of conceit. This is a hidden pride that conceals itself beneath the flesh. God is always faithful to point it out to me so that I can cut it out through the power of Jesus' shed blood on the cross.

Other subtle sins, such as jealousy, bitterness and resentment for things people have done or said in the past, can also eat away at us and steal our prayer power. In my own life, when I find my patience being tested or I begin thinking thoughts that I want to forget, the sin of bitterness can creep in. I have formulated the following confession of sin, based on portions of Scripture (see Matt. 5:43-45; 1 Cor. 13:4-7; Phil. 2:3), to help fortify myself against this subtlety of bitterness:

> I will strive to be patient and kind, not jealous or boastful or proud or rude. I will not demand my own way, be irritable, or keep a record of being wronged. I will not rejoice about injustice but will rejoice whenever the truth wins out. I will never give up and never lose faith. I will always be hopeful and endure through every circumstance. I will turn the other cheek, give up my coat, allow myself to be wronged, walk the extra mile, give when asked, love my enemies, bless those that curse me, do good to those that hate me, and pray for those who despitefully use me and persecute me. As much as is possible, I will be at peace with all people. I will do nothing out of conceit but will strive to esteem others better than myself. I am able to do these things not in my own strength but because I can do all things through Christ who strengthens me.

I confess my secret sins, because I know that if I have sin in my heart, I have God's promise that He will not hear me: "If I regard iniquity in my heart, the Lord will not hear" (Ps. 66:18). And I *want* to be heard. So, I first pray for what is close to my heart: the salvation of my loved ones. I make sure that I don't fret about it. I don't panic. I rest in God's faithfulness and thank Him that whatsoever I ask in prayer, believing, I shall receive.

I also pray for laborers who will tell others about the only way to salvation. Jesus told us that there were many who were ready for salvation but that there were few to help them get to that point, and that we were to pray for more laborers (see Matt. 9:37-38). The fact that you are reading this book is an answer to my prayers. So pray for God to raise up laborers who will forget about themselves and reach out to the lost. May you see the answer to your prayers as you plead for more laborers as well.

I also pray for wisdom. God gave Solomon wisdom when he asked for it, and He promises to give us wisdom when we ask for it. So I ask for wisdom, because I need it. I need it because I am regularly doing and saying dumb things. But I say that with a qualification.

For example, I don't have a vehicle, and when I occasionally get to drive Sue's van, I almost always listen to a well-known female talk show host. People call in to tell her personal, intimate problems (in front of 20 million listeners) because they need solutions. I listen to the problem and think to myself that if I were the host, I would say, *"Wow. That's too bad. I would be really depressed about that. Thanks for your call."* Click. But this host has an answer for every problem. As soon as she gives it, I think, *Man, is that wisdom! She's a modern Solomon. Why didn't I think of that? I am so dumb.* But then I hear her blaspheme, and I think, *This woman hasn't begun to be wise. The fear of the Lord is the beginning of wisdom.*

There is a wisdom that's of this world and there is a wisdom that's of God, and it's important for us to realize that the dumbest of Christians is a thousand times wiser than the wisest of this world. Why? Because we fear God, we seek God's kingdom first and His righteousness, we seek treasures in heaven and not on this earth, and we love Jesus Christ. The world doesn't see us as having wise priorities, but that will all change on Judgment Day.

So pray for wisdom. One of the wisest things we can do is seek the lost: "He who wins souls is wise" (Prov. 11:30).

DISCIPLINE

A firefighter must have discipline. This is because of the nature of his work. Discipline means speed, and speed can mean the saving of a human life. His boots are clean and at the ready. The equipment is checked and ready. His mind and body are ready. He must remain alert, and that means that he disciplines himself to eat and sleep well. He can't afford to be lazy and fat. Have you ever seen a slow-moving and fat firefighter? It just doesn't happen. Self-indulgence is beneath his calling. He needs to be able to move quickly and be in the best of shape. And that takes discipline.

The heart of Christianity is a mental and physical discipline. This is why followers of Jesus Christ are called "disciples" of Christ. Christians discipline themselves to His every word (see John 8:31-32). They are disciplined in mind and body because they need to be quick on their feet. So they feed on His Word daily, without fail. That's the healthy diet for Christians, and it is from the Word that they gain their energy.

Christians also exercise themselves to godliness. Sin makes them slow and weak. It's their kryptonite. They wait on the Lord so that He can renew their strength and make them mount up with wings like an eagle's. They must be strong in the Lord and in the power of His might, because the time may come when they need that strength to save someone's life.

There are a thousand other things they could be doing rather than seeking God in prayer, but they don't do them because they must pray. For they know that without the power of prayer, they will be ineffective in the greatest of all causes—the saving of human life from the fires of hell.

—Kirk Cameron

Basil and His Bible

I was in Florida on a friend's boat for a day. As we approached a wharf, I threw a rope to a man I had never met, and then jumped off the boat onto the wharf. I extended my hand and said, "Hi, I'm Ray." He responded by telling me that his name was Basil. I handed him a million-dollar bill tract and said, "It's a gospel tract." A moment later, I said, "Hey, Basil. I have a question for you. What do you think happens after someone dies?" I didn't live the Christian life before him to earn the right to witness. I imitated Jesus. He didn't wait too long before He spoke to the woman at the well (see John 4). I jumped in quickly, and I used words, because they were necessary.

After I went through the Ten Commandments with Basil, I shared the gospel. He was unsaved but open to hearing about salvation. So I asked, "Do you read your Bible?" He said, "No, but I pray every day." I said, "Basil, prayer is *you* talking to God. The Bible is *God* talking to you. You need to be slow to speak and swift to hear. Stop talking and listen to what God wants you to do, because your eternity depends on it."

Did you know the content of your prayers reveals something about you? What do you pray for? Is it selfish or selfless? Are you asking for God's blessing on yourself or do your prayers reflect that you are seeking first the kingdom of God and His righteousness?

There are many who pray selfless prayers. They desperately want to see revival, and so they pray. That's wonderful. God bless them. But it's important to remember that Jesus didn't say, "Go into all the world and pray," or, "Go into all the world and sign petitions." He said, "Go into all the world and preach the gospel to every creature." This is because God has chosen the foolishness of preaching to save those who believe. Prayer without obedience toward the Great Commission equals words without works. It equates to drawing near to God with our lips but having a heart that isn't running to do His will. Our lips should express what's in our heart. We should be praying, "Here I am, Lord. Send me."

The late pastor and author A.W. Tozer warned:

Have you noticed how much praying for revival has been going on of late—and how little revival has resulted? Considering the volume of prayer that is ascending these days, rivers of revival should be flowing in blessing throughout the land. That no such results are in evidence should not discourage us; rather it should stir us to find out why our prayers are not answered. . . . I believe our problem is that we have been trying to substitute praying for obeying; and it simply will not work. . . . Prayer is never an acceptable substitute for obedience. The sovereign Lord accepts no offering from His creatures that is not accompanied by obedience. To pray for revival while ignoring or actually flouting the plain precept laid down in the Scriptures is to waste a lot of words and get nothing for our trouble.

So pray without ceasing, and be just as zealous with your evangelism. Seek the lost without ceasing. Witness like there is no tomorrow. One day you will be right. You will have eternity to rest, but now you must speak.

Work in Quiet Urgency

I stood by the counter at the Long Beach Airport in a state of unbelief. It was Saturday night and I was due to speak at a church just north of San Francisco on Sunday morning, but my flight had been cancelled. Airlines often do that to save money. After all, why send a flight off with hardly anyone on board? It's financially sensible to cancel it and rebook the customer on a later flight. The airline said that they had notified me via email, but no one in our office remembered getting such a message. There was a chance, though, that if I took an early Sunday morning flight, I could make it to the service. I was due to speak at 10:00 A.M. The airline said they could get me to San Francisco at 9:18 A.M. There was a 30-minute drive after that, so I called the pastor to see if he wanted to take that risk. He did, so I rebooked my flight.

As soon as I exited the plane in San Francisco, I ran through the airport and jumped into a waiting car. I threw my bags in the back, and the driver put his foot down as much as his conscience would allow. Thirty or so minutes later, we drove into the church parking lot, where five men were waiting. As we walked briskly toward the church, the soundman clipped a microphone onto my shirt and my belt. We entered the church doors and walked across the lobby, where I heard the pastor say, "Here he is! I have never met him, but let's welcome Ray Comfort." The timing was amazing.

That incident reminded me of the urgency of both our mission and the hour in which we live. We need to evangelize the lost with a quiet urgency. Although I know that God is sovereign and will save whom He will, I also know that we are called to preach like dying men and work while it is yet day, for the time will come when the door of God's mercy will close. This is the type of urgency I see demonstrated in the book of Acts.

Someone once asked me if I ever get a special urge to share the gospel with someone. I told them that I get a special urge to share it with *everyone*. I have never met anyone, even the angriest of hecklers or the most ardent of atheists, of whom I thought to myself, *You can go to hell. I don't care.* Jesus said, "Go into all the world and preach the gospel to every creature." I can't get around the words "*all* the world" and "*every* creature." To me, that seems to say "all" the world and "every" creature.

God Can Use Your Imperfection

Imagine if a firefighter started to climb the ladder toward a burning window and then stopped, looked up and called out, "Lady, I have been doing some soul searching as I climbed up. I am not doing this out of a pure motive. It's all ego. Yes, I know that it looks like I am being courageous, but I just wanted to look good—to be a hero—to get my face in the newspapers. That's not good. I'm sorry, but I'm going to have to let you and your precious kids burn to death." That woman wouldn't care less why the firefighter rescued her, as long as he rescued her. Here's the right motive for you as you rescue those who are lost:

> *And on some have compassion,* making a distinction; but others save with fear, pulling them out of the fire, hating even the garment defiled by the flesh (Jude 1:22-23, emphasis added).

Your motive should be pure compassion, but don't do too much self-searching while people are going to hell. Only God has pure compassion. You are human. Sin can get in and mess you up, but never let the fact that you are not God slow you down from doing His work. Just do it while there is still time. And if you have not been following His command to reach the lost because you are fearful of the reproach of the cross, perhaps you need to go somewhere and weep bitterly.

FOR HEAVEN'S APPLAUSE

A well-dressed figure walked briskly down the sidewalk, reveling in the sense of excitement in his heart. He was carrying the savings of a lifetime, and he had big plans. They were plans for his future and for the future of his beloved family. His family had trusted him to go into the city and invest everything they had accrued in a family business that would set them up for life. It was a sure thing.

Suddenly, two men stood in front of him. One held a knife, and the other lifted a piece of wood that looked like a baseball bat. *Thieves!* He had heard this was a bad area, but he hadn't expected trouble in broad daylight.

As he stood paralyzed with terror, he sensed someone coming up behind him. He swung around, only to be greeted with a tremendous slam to his chest. As he bent over doubled, he felt a powerful blow to the side of his head, and then something smashed into his face. *These men were going kill him!* The ground seemed to rise up, and then darkness overtook him.

Some time later, the half-dead man opened his eyes. The thieves were gone, and so was his money. That was no surprise. He couldn't move. He could barely breathe, probably because his ribs were broken. Blood caked his mouth and his nose. His head throbbed, and the world around him seemed to spin.

As he lay on the sidewalk, he began to think about his plight. Few people came this way. The hot sun baked his skin. He could taste dirt mingled with blood. Instinctively he whispered, "Water!" Was he going to die here?

It seemed like an eternity before he heard someone approaching. He slowly lifted his head and tried to focus his eyes. The figure was wearing black—it was a priest, a man of God. As the priest came closer, he looked up at him and cried a pathetic, "Help me!" The priest stared back, and then walked around him and made his way quickly into the distance.

Another figure approached and did the same thing. He looked intently at the dying man and then went across to the other side of the street and disappeared. I will let Jesus finish the story:

> But a certain Samaritan, as he journeyed, came where he was. And when he saw him, he had compassion. So he went to him and bandaged his wounds, pouring on oil and wine; and he set him on his own animal, brought him to an inn, and took care of him. On the next day, when he departed, he took out two denarii, gave them to the innkeeper, and said to him, "Take care of him; and whatever more you spend, when I come again, I will repay you" (Luke 10:33-35).

I've taken some poetic license with the story because we don't know the details. But we *do* know that the beaten man was probably a Jew, that he was left for dead on the side of the road by thieves, and that a Samaritan (a group of people who had no dealings with the Jews) saw him. Despite the enmity between the Jews and the Samaritans, this Samaritan had a virtue the others lacked. He had *compassion*. That's what stopped him from crossing to the other side. Compassion wouldn't let him. Compassion led him to bandage the man, pour oil and wine on his wounds, and take him to an inn and say, "Whatever he spends, I will repay."

Compassion cost the rescuer. And it will cost you and me. Compassion will not let you see this half-dead world and pass by on the other side. It will tell you that the oil and wine of the gospel isn't just for you. It won't let you be guilty of the crime of "depraved indifference"—the crime of letting someone die when you can save him or her. Compassion will cost you time, money, energy, reputation and dignity.

Constrained by Compassion

When I found everlasting life in April of 1972, I could hardly believe that I had found an answer to death. It sent me delirious with joy, and at the same time sick with horror at the thought of a real place called hell.

In 1974, I began preaching open air in the heart of the city in which I lived, and I did it almost daily for 12 years.[1] There was no honorarium, no applause, no air conditioning or central heating, and no sound system. Many times, I became discouraged. I was mocked almost daily and subjected to indignities that I wouldn't mention in mixed company. But I kept going back, day after day— more than 3,000 times. Compassion cost me.

I have often been asked why I am so zealous to reach the lost. My answer is that I became a Christian. It's as simple as that. Before I was a Christian, I wanted to do my own will. After I was saved, I wanted to do God's will. I see myself as a *normal*, biblical Christian. There is nothing special about a Christian laying down his life to serve God.

When we moved from New Zealand to the United States in 1989, I preached the gospel for a year at the infamous MacArthur Park in downtown Los Angeles. Then I began taking a team to Santa Monica every Friday night for three and a half years. We traveled 60 miles to preach to this half-dead world. Compassion cost me. For two and a half years each weekday, my son-in-law ("E.Z.") and I preached to the crowds at the local courts. When we were stopped from doing that by a judge who didn't like what we were doing, I began to take a small team to preach at Huntington Beach every Saturday for years.

I would have preferred to stay at home with my wife, or watch sports on TV. I would have preferred to sit at my computer and write about reaching the lost. I would have preferred to just sit and do nothing, but compassion wouldn't let me.

Now, when I say that "compassion wouldn't let me," I'm not speaking of a deep love that comes from my human nature. It's not in me to go back day after day and preach the gospel to a world that isn't just passive to what I am saying but actually deeply offended by it. They *hate* the light. It is the love of Christ that constrains me. It is His love inside me—that is inside any believer—that pushes me to do that which I know I should.

How many of us would go out of our way as far as the "good" Samaritan did? Before I came to Christ, I hope that I would have stopped to help someone who had been beaten and left half dead on the side of the road. I hope that I would have taken him to a hospital or called an ambulance. But I doubt if I would have gone as far as saying, "Send me the bill." But that's what the Samaritan did. What's more, he did what the Law simply required of him—to love his neighbor as himself.

So, for you and me to lay down our lives for the lost is no big deal. It's what the Law of God requires of us. And when it's all said and done, as I lay my head on the pillow of my deathbed, I will whisper, "What else could I have done? Compassion cost God the blood of His Son, so laying down my life was my 'reasonable service.' I am nothing more than an unprofitable servant who one night in 1972 whispered, 'Not my will, Lord, but Yours be done.'"

Hot Chicks

Sue and I went to a store to purchase six more chickens on a hot day. Usually, the assistant would have to run around with a net to catch them. But not on this day, because the heat had made the chickens submissive. They just squatted on the ground, and she picked them up without any fuss.

The heat of tribulation tends to do that to us chickens. Trials tend to slow us down and bring us to our knees to the point that we are more willing to say, "Not my will, but Yours be done." Think about the times in life when things are going well. If we aren't in total submission to the Lord, those are the times when we get slack with prayer, quiet time, reading the Word and especially reaching out to the lost.

The Bible says that we enter the kingdom of God through much tribulation. Fiery trials tend to drive us closer to God. The winds of adversity make us send our roots deeper into God. However, with the clear mandate to reach the lost, trials shouldn't only take us to our knees, but also send us to the lost. This is what happened in the book of Acts.

Do you remember what happened when the heat of tribulation came on the Church in the form of a fiery Saul of Tarsus? It seems that the prospering Church had got a little slack. The Bible tells us that Saul created havoc in the Church, and those who were scattered went everywhere preaching the gospel to a dying world (see Acts 8:1-4).

If you are a follower of Jesus, you should be a fisher of men (see Mark 1:17), and if you are not, you are following Jesus at a distance and need to close the gap today. You need to have your Gethsemane experience. You are needed in these closing hours of time. You need to put this book down, get on your knees and whisper, "Lord, the thought of preaching the cross makes me sweat drops of blood in fear. Let this cup pass from me. Nevertheless, not my will, but Yours, be done."

As a follower of Jesus, when your speech betrays you and someone says, "You are one of them," may the string of your tongue be loosed. May you boldly say, "The Lord is my helper. I will not fear what man shall do to me!" (Heb. 13:6). And, like Esther of old, may you have the courage to say, "If I perish, I perish. I was born for such a time as this" (Esther 4:14).

THE QUESTION OF ETERNAL DESTINY

Hell is just a heartbeat away for the world. Such a thought should give each of us a sense of urgency to reach out to the unsaved. I have lost count of the biographical books I have read in which famous Christians tell their life's story *but never once* witness to a soul. Sure, they talk about God in a nice way and relate interesting stories, but it's as though no one is going to hell at all. They are arranging the furniture while the entire house is on fire and its occupants are still asleep.

Christians should be utterly unique in this dying world. They should be consumed with a mission. They should be like that resolute firefighter making his way through fire to rescue human beings from a burning building. If I want to express to someone that I am only human and have human weaknesses, I may say, "Listen, I put on my pants *one* leg at a time." But firefighters have put on their pants *two* legs at a time. They live with a unique sense of urgency, ready to rescue lives at a moment's notice. That is how every Christian should live. But most don't.

Other books I have read tell true stories of Christian missionaries who spent *years* with the indigenous peoples before they could even talk to them about salvation. It seems that they were of the mentality that they had to live with the lost, dress like them, eat and talk like them, build hospitals for them and try and civilize them *before* they had the right to speak to them about their eternal salvation. But what about the eternal destiny of those who died in their sins while all this was going on? If they died in their sins, their fate was sealed forever in hell.

It goes without saying that a missionary must be culturally sensitive, but when anyone gets a grip on biblical evangelism, he or she can speak almost immediately to any sinner in any part of the world *because God has given all nations the light of the conscience.* If I am in a foreign country and have a language interpreter, I can ask *anyone* what he or she thinks happens after death. All cultures have some belief about the subject, so I simply tell them what the Bible says—that they have to face the God of creation when they die and that His standard is the Law of God. I open up each of the Ten Commandments to show the nature of sin. Then I tell them of Judgment Day, the reality of hell, the glory of the cross and what Jesus' death, burial and resurrection means to them, and their need to repent of sin and have faith in Jesus alone to save them from eternal judgment. I leave the "results" up to God. I don't have to spend two years learning the culture to earn the right to share the gospel.

When we filmed the fourth season of our TV program *The Way of the Master*, I preached the biblical gospel in 13 countries in 13 days, and people in each country listened and understood the issues. I have seen the Law do its work in France, Hungary, Germany, England, Australia, India, New Zealand, Singapore, Japan and many other countries around the world. It is completely universal. What culture doesn't have a conscience?

The Full Life

If you begin to open-air preach, you will live a life that is somewhat reminiscent to the disciples in the book of Acts. Let me share a typical day with you.

I was passionately open-air preaching with my team at the base of the pier of Huntington Beach, California, when two fire trucks pulled up and parked about 50 feet in front of me. Their engines were running, but all eight firefighters just sat there and stared at me. It was very strange. My guess is that someone had called the fire department and told them there was a fire. They kept staring for a few minutes, and then they backed up and left. The incident reminded me of the words of John Wesley. He said, "Get on fire for God, and people will come to watch you burn." I guess he was right.

Some time later, a young man with a few tattoos, wearing his pants at half-mast, was standing in front of me. So I asked, "Where are you going when you die?" He said, "Heaven." When I asked his name, he said it was "Brian," so I asked, "Brian, why are you going to heaven?"

"Because I'm a Christian."

"Have you been born again?"

"Yes."

"When did you last read your Bible?"

"Last night."

"What did you read?"

"The Book of Moses."

The *Book of Moses* is a text published by The Church of Jesus Christ of Latter-day Saints and today is published as part of the *Pearl of Great Price.* Those who practice Mormonism consider it to be the translated writings of Moses. I didn't think that that was what Brian was meaning, so I asked, "And what did you read in the 'Book of Moses?' "

"The opening up of the Red Sea . . ."

"What chapter was that?"

"Ecclesiastics."

"You are you lying to me, aren't you, Brian?"

"Yes, I am. I did see the movie *The Prince of Egypt* though."

It would have been easy for me to give up when Brian said that he was a Christian and that he was reading the Word. But a genuine concern for the unsaved will urge us to make sure that someone isn't under deception. One way to do that is to ask if the person is reading the Bible. Few people who are in sin read the Bible, because God's Word accuses them of their sin, and that's not a pleasant feeling for a guilty sinner.

One thing you will get used to in open-air testimony is being around people who have had enough to drink to rid them of their inhibitions. This is what is commonly called being under "satonic" influence. Drunks often open themselves to the influence of demons, and one man I met on this day (who seemed to have had a few drinks) was extremely angry and very verbal. He kept hollering at me to get off my box, humble myself and start showing real love by helping people in a practical way rather than preaching at them about their sins.

He returned some time later and began to heckle my teammate Scotty. The man was still angry and almost got into a fight with a "helpful" Christian, who took it on himself to rebuke the man (which is not a wise thing to do). They were literally nose to nose, like a couple of angry pit bulls.

I then noticed that a Buddhist monk was listening as I spoke, so I asked him if he believed in God. He said that he did, but that it was tied up with "karma." I explained that God's "karma" is that He will punish sin with death and hell. Then I opened up the Ten Commandments, preached the cross and explained the necessity of repentance and faith.

There is a legitimate concern that such preaching may be construed as though I am condemning sincere religious people (such as a quiet-spoken Buddhist monk). However, I can get around this by explaining the function of "religion." Religion is man's efforts to try to get right with God, something man can never do. But the gospel does it for him. The gospel is unspeakably good news for Buddhists, Hindus, Moslems, Jews and Gentiles.

God Himself made a way for all mankind to be justified (to be made right with Him), and that way is through faith alone in the Savior (see John 14:6). People simply need to repent of their sin and transfer their faith in themselves (and in their works) into faith in Jesus Christ alone as their sole sin bearer. Then God will forgive their sins and grant them everlasting life.

Another man named Tom kept telling Scotty that he didn't believe what he was preaching. He said that the god *he* believed in wasn't at all condemning. After Scotty had finished speaking, he handed Tom's comment over to me to answer, and I told Tom that he was guilty of violating the second of the Ten Commandments. He didn't know what that command was, so I quoted the first, "You shall have no other gods before me," and then the second, "You shall not make yourself a graven image," to show it in context. He had another "god" in which he believed instead of the God who created him. He had made a god in his own image. His god was a figment of his imagination that he shaped to suit himself. His god had no moral dictate. Tom could do what he wanted morally and not make his god frown at all. Tom was an "idolater," and idolaters will not inherit the kingdom of God.

Practice What You Preach

Perhaps you are thinking that you could never do what I do. You could never talk with people about their eternal destiny because you are not quick on your feet. You are easily tongue-tied. But you are forgetting one thing: *God will help you.* Besides, one reason I can do it is because I have had lots of practice. You will learn to answer questions as they are asked of you. Sometimes you will have the answers, and sometimes you won't.

What marathon runner ever wins a race without practice? He or she started practicing one step at a time. You do the same, and step up to the plate (to deliberately mix metaphors). Have a swing at it. You aren't going to hit a home run the first time, but you will learn what to do the next time if someone throws you a curve-ball. What have you got to lose but your pride? And it is pride that is holding you back, isn't it? Besides, you are on the winning team. You really can't lose at all.

When you stand up to open-air preach, there will be times when only a handful of people will listen. Sometimes the crowd will grow in number to 100 or 200; other times it will stay at just 1 or 2 people. Don't let that discourage you. *Remember that you don't know who is listening.* That one person could be someone God is going to use to reach millions. Charles Spurgeon once spoke about a man who brought one such individual to Christ, and how that affected millions of other people:

> "He first found his own brother Simon" (John 1:41). This case is an excellent pattern of all cases where spiritual life

is vigorous. As soon as a man has found Christ, he begins to find others. I will not believe that you have tasted of the honey of the Gospel if you can eat it all yourself. True grace puts an end to all spiritual monopoly. Andrew first found his own brother Simon, and then others. Relationship has a very strong demand upon our first individual efforts.

Andrew, you did well to begin with Simon. I doubt whether there are not some Christians giving away tracts at other people's houses who would do well to give away a tract at their own—whether there are not some engaged in works of usefulness abroad who are neglecting their special sphere of usefulness at home. You may or may not be called to evangelize the people in any particular local-ity, but certainly you are called to see after your own ser-vants, your own kinsfolk and acquaintances.

Let your religion begin at home. Many tradesmen ex-port their best commodities—the Christian should not. He should have all his conversation everywhere of the best savour; but let him have a care to put forth the sweetest fruit of spiritual life and testimony in his own family. When Andrew went to find his brother, he little imagined how eminent Simon would become. Simon Peter was worth ten Andrews so far as we can gather from sacred history, and yet Andrew was instrumental in bringing him to Jesus. You may be very deficient in talent yourself, and yet you may be the means of drawing to Christ one who shall become eminent in grace and service.

Ah! Dear friend, you little know the possibilities which are in you. You may but speak a word to a child, and in that child there may be slumbering a noble heart which shall stir the Christian church in years to come. Andrew has only two talents, but he finds Peter. Go and do likewise.[1]

So what are you waiting for? Take courage and go find your Peter. How do you do that in a practical way? We will look at that in the next chapter.

FROM DARKNESS TO LIGHT

I was preparing to speak at a classy hotel in Southern California when I saw a well-dressed gentleman in his late fifties reading a newspaper. I have a gift of perception. I could see that he hated Christians. I could tell by the look on his face and his God-hating jaw line. He was reading his paper intently, and I knew that in the back of his mind he was thinking about how mad he would get if some religious fundamentalist tried to ram religion down his throat. I ignored my fears and thought about the man's salvation. Perhaps he was some Christian lady's husband, and she had pleaded with God for years to bring someone to witness to him. Or maybe he was some Christian's beloved dad. Even if he wasn't, how could I not be concerned about where he would spend eternity?

I went up to the man, handed him a million-dollar bill tract and said, "Did you get your million? It will help with gas prices." He smiled, took it and said, "This is interesting." I then asked, "So, what do you think of the economy?" For the next five minutes, I heard every cussword in the book as he talked about how bad it was. Then I introduced myself, and I learned that his name was John. I said, "Are you a lawyer?" He was. I then said, "John, I have a question for you. What do you think happens when someone dies?"

I was surprised (although it often happens) that there was no mention of my huge change in the subject of our conversation. He didn't say, "Well, that is a bit off the wall. Here I am talking about politics and you go and ask about my personal religious beliefs." There was nothing like that.

This is because that question is extremely inoffensive. Think about it: I haven't mentioned God, Jesus, the Bible, sin, righteousness, judgment, heaven or hell. I simply asked him for his opinion (his favorite subject) on something that is a mystery to those who don't know the Lord.

John simply said, "I don't know. I don't think there's anything afterwards. My ego would like to think there is something. But, no, I don't think there is anything. I had a friend once who was shot in war. He came really close to death, and he said that when you are dead, you are dead."

I responded, "How would he know?"

"You're right," John said. "He wouldn't know."

"Do you think you are a good person?" I asked.

"Well, I'm a bit of good and a bit of bad."

"Let's see if that's true. I will put you on the stand and examine you. All I want from you is the truth, the whole truth and nothing but the truth, so help you God. Okay?"

"Okay."

"How many lies have you told in your life?"

"About a million."

"What do you call someone who tells lies?"

"A liar."

Now, for years I asked, "Have you ever told a lie?" and I would find that it often caused a problem for me, because when I asked what someone who told lies was called, he or she would say, "Well, it was just one or two. And they were 'white' lies, and you can't really call someone a 'liar' in that case." However, the question, "How many lies do you think you have told in your whole life?" is completely nonthreatening. There is no mention of God, morality or personal responsibility, so people usually boast unashamedly and say "lots" or "I have lost count" or "millions." That was the case with the lawyer. After such a blatant admission, rarely do people try to justify their sins.

"Have you ever stolen anything in your life, even if it was small?" I asked.

"When I was young."

"What do you call someone who steals things?"

"A thief."

"Have you ever used God's name in vain?"

"Yes."

"Jesus said, 'Whoever looks at a women to lust for her has already committed adultery with her in his heart' (Matt. 5:28). Have you ever looked at a woman with lust?"

"Sure have. Many times."

"So, John, by your own admission (I'm not judging you), you are a lying, thieving, blasphemous adulterer at heart, and we've only looked at four of the Ten Commandments. If God were to judge you by the Ten Commandments on the Day of Judgment, would you be innocent or guilty?"

At this point, John tried to justify himself by saying, "But you are not taking the balance into account. I have done some good things in my life."

"Okay. You're a lawyer. Let's take this to civil law. Answer me this: If I had raped a women and then killed her and said, 'Judge, I admit my guilt, but you're not taking the balance into account. I have been nice to many ladies, and I've given to charity,' what would the judge say?"

John didn't let me finish. He saw the point. A good judge would never let a criminal go just because he had done some good deeds. He would judge according to the crime committed, because a good judge must uphold justice.

When I asked, "Would you deserve heaven or hell?" John said that he couldn't believe in the concept of hell and that he had to go. He was under extreme conviction of sin, and as he tried to quickly exit the scene, I walked alongside him for a moment saying that God was good and He would see that justice was done.

I thanked John for listening to me, and we parted company.

Did I Fail?

Was that encounter a success when the man didn't even hear the gospel? The consoling answer lies in Scripture. There, we see a well-to-do man walk away from Jesus without hearing the gospel. This is what happened:

> Now as He was going out on the road, one came running, knelt before Him, and asked Him, "Good Teacher, what shall I do that I may inherit eternal life?"
>
> So Jesus said to him, "Why do you call Me good? No one is good but One, that is, God. You know the commandments: 'Do not commit adultery,' 'Do not murder,' 'Do not steal,' 'Do not bear false witness,' 'Do not defraud,' 'Honor your father and your mother.'"

And he answered and said to Him, "Teacher, all these things I have kept from my youth."

Then Jesus, looking at him, loved him, and said to him, "One thing you lack: Go your way, sell whatever you have and give to the poor, and you will have treasure in heaven; and come, take up the cross, and follow Me."

But he was sad at this word, and went away sorrowful, for he had great possessions (Mark 10:17-22).

Jesus didn't change the conditions of salvation. This man loved his money more than he loved God. To be saved he had to get rid of his money. He had violated the first of the Ten Commandments, but he left Jesus that day, knowing that fact. The encounter was a success because even though the rich young man just walked away, he understood what he would have to do to come to salvation.

Imagine if a man who thought he was healthy visited a doctor who took the time to show him that he had a terminal disease. Suppose the man listened and got so upset that he walked out of the doctor's office. What more could the doctor do? He had been faithful to tell the man the truth, and it was his hope that the man would seek further help as he thought about his condition. But the doctor's conscience was clear. He had done the right thing.

My time with John the lawyer was worthwhile because he listened and heard that he had sinned against God. My confidence is that God knows him by name. He knows how many hairs are on John's head, and He is quite capable of bringing someone else to John at the right time to share the cure of the cross with him. In the meantime, I will pray for him.

FAITHFULNESS

A firefighter must be a man of his word. If he says that he will be there, he will be there. If he says that he will do something, he will do it. Imagine calling an emergency number to request help and finding that the firefighters don't bother to show up. It's unthinkable.

The Christian must also be a person of his word. If he says he will do something, he will do it. If he says he will be on time, he will keep it to the second, if possible. He never trivializes not telling the truth by calling it a "fib" or a "white lie." He must be found faithful, because he is employed to do a job for God, who is utterly faithful to His word.

The Scriptures tell us, "Confidence in an unfaithful man in time of trouble is like a bad tooth and a foot out of joint" (Prov. 25:19). A broken tooth or a foot out of joint isn't too much trouble until pressure is applied to it. And it's when the pressure comes on that a Christian needs to be faithful. We are told, "Most men will proclaim each his own goodness, but who can find a faithful man?" (Prov. 20:6).

Men and women who keep their word are few and far between. Be one of them.

—Kirk Cameron

The Depth of the Penalty

I understand John when he says that it is hard to believe in the concept of hell. The existence of hell is unreasonable at first thought. However, there is a wonderful analogy I heard that explains why sin has such a harsh penalty.

If I lie to my dog, it's no big deal. If I lie to my wife, I may find myself sleeping on the couch for the night. If I lie to a police officer, I may find myself with a big fine or jail time. But if I lie under oath to a Supreme Court judge, I am in serious trouble. I will go to prison for a long time. It's just a lie, but the penalty *increases* according to whom I am telling the lie.

The Bible tells us that when we lie, we sin against God (see Ps. 51:4). We transgress *His* Law, and that is extremely serious. Scripture tells us that "lying lips are an abomination to the LORD" (Prov. 12:22). Lying is so serious that God killed a couple because they just told one lie (see Acts 5:1-11). Look at the penalty for lying: "All liars shall have their part in the lake of fire" (Rev. 21:8).

We trivialize lying by calling it a "fib" or a "white lie." That's not what God calls it.

When John the lawyer began to see his sin in its true light, he wanted to run from the courtroom. If he had heard the good news of God's mercy, any repentance would have been superficial. For repentance to be genuine, there must be godly sorrow. Look at how David owned his sin rather than blaming others or justifying himself after Nathan rebuked him for murder and adultery:

Have mercy upon me, O God,
According to Your lovingkindness;
According to the multitude of Your tender mercies,
Blot out my transgressions.
Wash me thoroughly from my iniquity,
And cleanse me from my sin.

For I acknowledge my transgressions,
And my sin is always before me.
Against You, You only, have I sinned,
And done this evil in Your sight—
That You may be found just when You speak,
And blameless when You judge (Ps. 51:1-4).

An email I received from a man named Patrick McDonnell sums it up well: "I think it is effective to help people understand repentance from a more relational perspective, similar to the remorse and commitment an unfaithful spouse would have to show to his or her marriage partner if he or she wanted the relationship to be restored. It is interesting that loving sin and the world is like committing adultery against God Himself according to James, Isaiah, and Jeremiah. When I ask people if they would forgive an unfaithful spouse if the apology were something lame like, 'Yea, I'm sorry, I'll try not to do it again, but all of my friends cheat on their spouses once in a while,' they are quick to say, 'No way, the person would have to be totally broken over what they did and be willing to never do it again for me to even consider forgiving them.' How easy it is at that point for them to realize that God demands nothing less to extend His forgiveness to someone who has denied Him the exclusive love that is due to Him."

THEY NEED
TO HEAR THE
MORAL LAW

As I mentioned earlier, I believe that we are seeing Bible prophecy being fulfilled before our very eyes. These are certainly perilous times. Men's hearts *are* failing them for fear of what's coming on the earth. There are suicide bombings and terrorism. Nation is rising against nation and kingdom against kingdom. The neighbors of Israel are boldly escalating their hatred of the Jews. Lawlessness and the love of sin abound on every side. Economies are collapsing, and as I watch political leaders try to keep a brave face, I can see fear deep in their eyes. I think of how they fail to even acknowledge the God who gave them life, and I think of the psalmist's prayer, "Arise, O LORD; do not let man prevail; let the nations be judged in your sight. Put them in fear, O LORD: that the nations may know themselves to be but men" (Ps. 9:19-20).

In the midst of speaking about the dark and seeing the frightening signs of the end of the age, Jesus has shone a beacon of wonderful light: "And this gospel of the kingdom shall be preached in all the world as a witness to all the nations, and then the end will come" (Matt. 24:14). You and I can be part of fulfilling Bible prophecy. God has entrusted us (as the Church) to be lighthouse keepers, especially at the end of this age. We are to steer a perishing world into the God-given safe-haven of salvation in Jesus Christ. So it's important for us to make sure we show our brilliance by embracing the work that God has called us to do. If ever we were needed, it's now.

Maybe it's not practical for you to open-air preach. Maybe you're a stay-at-home mom and your daily responsibilities have stopped you from laboring for God. Or maybe as a husband or father your time is consumed in just making sure your family has food on the table. Then cut your cloth to fit. Do what you can. Carry gospel tracts with you and look for opportunities to speak up boldly to make known the mystery of the gospel. How do you do that? I have a way that will make it easy for you.

Questions That Lead to the Gospel

I have experimented for years with how to make a smooth transition into the message of the gospel when talking with the lost. By the grace of God, I have learned to bring up the subject of the gospel in a way that helps dissipate my fear. It means that I can bring up the things of God without bringing up the things that can potentially cause contention—words such as "hell," "Judgment Day," "sin," "righteousness," "the Bible," "God," "Jesus," and "the cross."

Let's be honest about witnessing. Most of us would prefer a root cannel. Our fears fuel our minds to imagine the worst. When we look at a potential "victim," we think that the moment the things of God are mentioned, he or she will become a violent monster. So here is a fear-dissipating plan: Ask the person what he or she thinks happens when someone dies. Get this thought permanently fixed into your mind: *There's nothing offensive about that question.*

Think of how you would have responded to this question before you came to the faith. Would it have made you angry? Of course not. It's not loaded, so it has no potential to cause an explosion of any sort. You are simply asking for the person's opinion, and most people will readily give it by answering something like, "I'm not sure," or, "Everyone goes to heaven." The pleasant tone of his or her answer will immediately get rid of the fear that has been whispering to you. All you need to do is be ready with questions such as, "Do you think about it much?" You will often hear replies such as, "All the time." Then be ready with, "Are you afraid of dying?" and, "Do you think you will go to heaven?"

So, what do you say? Are you willing to completely surrender yourself to the most worthy cause on earth? Will you enlist without reservation to fight the *good* fight of faith? Ours is the most noble of battles. We are fighting for the eternal salvation of every human being's most precious possession.

Extending the Conversation

I sat next to a man named Joe who was involved in the financial side of a well-known national corporation. I knew that he was pretty intelligent when I asked him a few trick questions just to fill the time and he answered them correctly. The first was, "How many U. S. presidents are not buried in the United States?" In case you don't know, at present there are five: Jimmy Carter, George Bush Senior, George Bush Junior, Bill Clinton and Barack Obama (time will change the answer). The second question I asked was, "What was the highest mountain on earth before Mount Everest was discovered?" He knew that it was Mount Everest. It's always been the highest. He was one sharp cookie.

When I asked Joe what he thought happens after someone dies, he said that he wasn't an atheist but that he didn't believe in an afterlife. There was no heaven and no hell. So that was the end of the conversation, right? What can you say next if someone doesn't believe in heaven or hell?

Actually, there is a way to extend the conversation. I asked Joe to imagine that there was a heaven, and I asked if he thought he was good enough to go there. Did he think that he was a good person? The conversation went like this:

"I'm a very good person," he said.

I responded by saying, "Let's go through some of the Ten Commandments to see if you are, and if you will make it to heaven. How many lies have you told in your life?"

It turned out that he was a liar, a thief, a blasphemer and had committed adultery in his heart many times. I explained the cross, the necessity of repentance and faith and thanked him for listening to me.

About 30 minutes later, he started up the conversation again.

"I have a question for you," he said. "Why is it that Christianity says that people from all other religions are going to hell?"

"All other religions are what are called 'work-righteousness' religions. They think they have to do something to earn everlasting life. The Moslem prays five times a day, fasts and so on. The Hindu fasts, prays, lies on beds of nails . . . the thing that changes the equation is God's Law. It shows us that we are not simply unfortunate human beings trying to make our way through this life but also that we are wicked criminals in the sight of a holy God. So our 'good' works suddenly are not good works, but are actually attempts to bribe the Judge of the Universe. The Bible warns that 'the sacrifice of the wicked is an abomination to the LORD' (Prov. 15:9). He will not be bribed. But in Christianity, God provided a way for all humanity—the Moslem, the Hindu, the Buddhist, the Jew and the Gentile—to be saved. The offer of everlasting life comes from the mercy of the Judge—as a free gift. It is universal. 'Whosoever will,' may come."

Joe thought for a moment and then said, "I don't accept that. It seems unfair to me that it is exclusive."

"You mean because Jesus said He was the only way to God?"

"Yes."

"Do you think that Christianity is 'intolerant?'"

"Yes, I do."

"So, you are being intolerant of Christianity. You are doing what you are accusing Christianity of doing. Being intolerant."

"No, no, not at all. I was just wondering . . ."

For the next hour or so, Joe asked many questions. He listened thoughtfully and took a "What Hollywood Believes" CD and a copy of *The Way of the Master New Testament*. At the end of the flight, he thanked me for the conversation and said that he had learned a lot.

So, although it seemed like the end of our conversation when Joe said he didn't believe in heaven and hell, it really wasn't. Likewise, if someone you are talking to doesn't believe, just have him or her imagine that there is a heaven. It will be easy if he or she tries, and it will open up a door to that person's heart. Always remember that you are dealing with those of whom the Bible says are blind. You want them to know that there is another world, so speak, to their God-given imagination, and that will give you the opportunity to speak to their God-given conscience.

What Sin Causes

Jesus said that He is the Light of the World and that if we follow Him we will not walk in darkness but have the light of life (see John 8:12). We are no longer living in the darkness of ignorance, as is this sinful world. We know why terrible things are coming onto the face of this earth. It is all happening because of something called "sin," and as the Church, we need to know how to articulate this truth. America (and the rest of the world) needs to speak with a clear voice, saying, "This is the way!"

So what should we say? Isaiah 40:6-10 tells us the following:

> The voice said, "Cry out!" And he said, "What shall I cry?" "All flesh is grass, and all its loveliness is like the flower of the field. The grass withers, the flower fades, because the breath of the LORD blows upon it; surely the people are grass. The grass withers, the flower fades, but the word of our God stands forever." O Zion, you who bring good tidings, get up into the high mountain; O Jerusalem, you who bring good tidings, lift up your voice with strength, lift it up, be not afraid; say to the cities of Judah, "Behold your God!" Behold, the Lord GOD shall come with a strong hand, and His arm shall rule for Him; behold, His reward is with Him, and His work before Him.

There are several words that are currently dominating the contemporary secular news media in the United States: recession, depression, gas and food prices, bank loans, inflation and debt. We are the only nation on earth that has "In God We Trust" inscribed on our dollar bill, but that dollar is shrinking daily. It doesn't buy what it once did. Why is this happening? We are going to look at this issue in the light of Scripture so that you will know what to say when you lift up your voice.

God warned Israel that if they failed to trust in Him, they would lose His blessing and would become in debt to the foreigner. "He shall lend to you, but you shall not lend to him; he shall be the head, and you shall be the tail" (Deut. 28:44). He said that they would also have droughts and incurable diseases and that foreigners would fill the land.

Think of what's happening to America. Our national debt is more than 11 trillion dollars, and growing daily. Much of this debt is to foreign nations.[1] More than 1,000,000 Americans will get cancer in the next year.[2] We have terrible droughts, and yet we have continual massive floods. We are also plagued with devastating hurricanes and killer tornadoes. These things are not evidences of God's blessing. So why are they happening to us? Aren't we a morally good nation? Don't we trust in God? Before you answer, here are some statistics for you to consider:

- Between 1997 to 2007, approximately 180,000 people were murdered in the United States.[3]
- More than 50 million babies have been aborted since Roe v. Wade.[4]
- Of married couples, 45 to 55 percent of women and 50 to 60 percent of men admit to having an affair at some point in their marital relationship. Five million unwed couples live together.[5]
- By the age of 19, 75 percent of women and 80 percent of men have had premarital sex.[6]
- One-third of births to women aged 25 to 29 years were out of wedlock.[7]

- 1 in 4 teenage girls has a sexually transmitted disease.[8]
- Americans spend up to 4 billion dollars annually on pornography.[9]
- We have more than 2 million people in prison—the highest number in the world.[10]
- Surveys reveal that 91 percent of all people lie regularly.[11]

All this, and yet the idea that we have somehow offended God is unthinkable to most people. Rather, we blame the economy, politicians, pesticides, global warming, global cooling, El Niño, Mother Nature—anything but ourselves and our relationship to God. Why is this? Let's look at that next.

THE "FINE" HAS BEEN PAID!

In the previous chapter, I listed a number of our national sins that were transgressions against God's moral Law. It is the Law's function to bring the knowledge of sin to an individual and to a nation (see Rom. 3:20). Without the Law, we have no understanding of the true nature of sin. Paul said, "I would not have known sin except through the law" (Rom. 7:7).

Think of King David when he sinned with Bathsheba. He violated the Ten Commandments when he lusted after his neighbor's wife, lived a lie, stole her, committed adultery, committed murder, dishonored his parents and caused the enemies of God to blaspheme His name. The nature of his sin revealed that his image of God was erroneous, and he certainly didn't put God first in his affections.

While the world would say that King David was just a victim of his own moral weaknesses, the truth is that he was a covetous man whose greed took him deeply into sin. But it seems David wasn't too concerned about what he had done. It was no big deal. So God commissioned the prophet Nathan to reprove King David. What did Nathan do? Did he boldly stand before the king and say, "God has a wonderful plan"? Why would he say that? That would make no sense. David was a criminal who had committed *very* serious crimes. He had violated the moral Law and greatly offended God. So it would be ridiculous to present him with an offer of some sort of lifestyle improvement.

Instead, Nathan told David a story about a man who stole another man's lamb. When the king became indignant against the man, Nathan said, "*You* are the man! Why have you despised the Commandment of the Lord!" David was horrified and cried, "I have sinned against God!" And once David acknowledged his sins, then came the good news of God's mercy: "Nathan said to David, 'The LORD also has put away your sin; you shall not die'" (2 Sam. 12:13).

If you have had any experience at all in talking with the lost, you will know that they seek to justify their sin. They trivialize sin, blame others or spread the blame by saying that "*everyone* lies . . . or steals." But look at the fruit of Nathan's rebuke. Look at how David *owns* his sin in his penitent prayer. Count the times he says "me" and "my" in reference to his personal transgressions once he realizes that he has offended God:

> Have mercy upon me, O God, according to Your loving-kindness; according to the multitude of Your tender mercies, blot out my transgressions. Wash me thoroughly from my iniquity, and cleanse me from my sin. For I acknowledge my transgressions, and my sin is always before me. Against You, You only, have I sinned, and done this evil in Your sight—that You may be found just when You speak, and blameless when You judge (Ps. 51:1-4).

When you and I take someone through the Ten Commandments, God's moral Law shows them that they have greatly offended Him. It reveals to them that God is perfect, holy, just and good. That's why Jesus used the Law when speaking to the rich young ruler in Mark 10:18-19.

However, there are some who maintain that sinners don't need to hear the Law because they already know they are sinners. As we have seen earlier, they also maintain that it's not our job to point out sin. That's the job of the Holy Spirit. But look at how the apostle Paul addresses sinners, using the Law:

> You, therefore, who teach another, do you not teach yourself? You who preach that a man should not steal, do you steal? You who say, "Do not commit adultery," do you commit adultery? You who abhor idols, do you rob temples? You who make your boast in the law, do you dishonor God through breaking the law? For "the name of God is blasphemed among the Gentiles because of you," as it is written (Rom. 2:21-24).

According to Scripture, it's not true that sinners know the nature of sin. Look at Paul's own testimony in Romans 7:7:

> What shall we say then? Is the law sin? Certainly not! On the contrary, I would not have known sin except through the law. For I would not have known covetousness unless the law had said, "You shall not covet."

All you have to do to see the reality of what Scripture is saying is ask an unsaved person if he thinks he is a good person. He will almost always say, "I'm a very good person" (see Prov. 20:6). This is because that person is ignorant of God's perfect standard of righteousness. He measures himself by his own low moral standard and comes up clean in his own eyes. This is why he needs the Law. It's like a mirror that reflects the truth to him.

Yes, the Holy Spirit *does* convict of sin, but if you make the mistake of leaving out the Law, there will be no conviction of sin, and you will rob the gospel of its power. You will remove the God-given bow from the arrow, which will leave the gospel with no point. It seems foolish that someone would pay a fine if that person didn't know that he or she had broken the Law. The sinner concludes, "Why do I need a Savior if I'm a good person?"

When Paul took his hearers through each commandment and said, "Do you steal?" "Do you commit adultery?" he was in essence saying, "*You* are the man!" as Nathan did with David. He was personalizing sin so that the sinner would cry out (like David) for mercy. The famous Bible commentator Matthew Henry said, "Of this excellent use is the Law: it converts the soul, opens the eyes, prepares the way of the Lord."[1]

But How Could a Loving God . . .

How often we hear the world say that a loving God would never create hell. This is because when the Law is set aside, judgment makes no sense. It paints God (not the sinner) as the criminal. The full implication is that if a loving God created hell, He wouldn't be loving; He would be evil. The God of the Bible created hell, *therefore*, the God that the Bible portrays is evil.

However, bring the moral Law back in and the situation changes radically. Imagine if you knew of a judge who turned a blind eye when he saw a murder being committed. He had no desire to see that justice was done. Would he be a good judge? Obviously, he would be evil and should be brought to justice himself. A good judge must do everything he can to see that justice is done.

Do you remember from the last chapter how many murders took place in the United States during 1997 to 2007? There were about 180,000. But did you also know that there is only a 40 percent success rate in homicide investigations?[2] That means that during that 10 years, 80,000 people got away with murder. Men raped women, strangled them, cut up their bodies and put them in acid and poured them down the drain. No body, no conviction.

God is omniscient. He sees every murder that takes place. We are told in Scripture that nothing is hidden from His eyes. *Nothing.* So, if God is good, should He just look the other way? If He did, He wouldn't be good; He would be evil. Like the judge who turned a blind eye, He should be brought to justice Himself.

We know intuitively that God is good. However, the Bible tells us that He is so good that He will not only punish murderers but also punish those who *desired* to commit murder but never had opportunity to fulfill their wicked heart's desire. He will punish rapists, thieves, liars, fornicators and those who harbor feelings of lust, jealousy, hatred, greed and envy. He will bring to justice every secret thing—whether it is good or evil.

So when we bring in the Law, it shows that man is the criminal and His Creator is a judge who is perfect, holy, just and good. That makes a thinking person say, "How can there *not* be a hell?" Common sense concludes that there must be divine retribution for injustice.

But listen to our popular preachers. They are not "warning every man, that [they] might present every man perfect in Christ Jesus" (Col. 1:28). They preach as though all is well between heaven and earth. It was Martin Luther who said, "The first duty of the gospel preacher is to declare God's Law and show the nature of sin." That's what's wrong with this nation. There is no opening up of God's Law, and when you leave out the Law, man is just a victim of his own moral weaknesses. Humanity finds itself with the same flippant attitude that David had toward his terrible sin. Popular preachers reproduce their own kind in the pews, and few care about the lost. They don't see God as being perfect, holy, just and good, because the Law has never been used to bring the knowledge of sin. They not only lack concern for humanity's salvation but also lack gratitude for their own professed salvation.

Puffed Up by Pride

Let's take a look at what Jesus said about this kind of attitude in the Bible.[4] In Luke 13:18, Jesus said that the kingdom of God is like a mustard seed that a man put in his garden. It grew and became a large tree, and the birds of the air nested in its branches. Then He said that the kingdom of heaven "is like leaven, which a woman took and hid in three measures of meal till it was all leavened" (v. 21). In Exodus 12:15-21, the children of Israel were commanded to eat only unleavened bread. If anyone ate bread that contained leaven, they were to be "cut off from Israel" (v. 15). Later, when Jesus fed the 4,000 (see Mark 8:1-10) and the Pharisees came to Him and demanded a "sign" from heaven (see v. 11), Jesus told His disciples that they should "beware of the leaven of the Pharisees and the leaven of Herod" (v. 15). In Matthew's Gospel, we see that He also included the Sadducees (see Matt. 16:1). The disciples thought that He was chiding them for forgetting to take some bread with them, but when they began to question why He had spoke of the leaven, Jesus said:

"Why do you reason because you have no bread? Do you not yet perceive nor understand? Is your heart still hardened? Having eyes, do you not see? And having ears, do you not hear? And do you not remember? When I broke the five loaves for the five thousand, how many baskets full of fragments did you take up?" They said to Him, "Twelve." "Also, when I broke the seven for the four thousand, how many large baskets full of fragments did you take up?" And they said, "Seven." So He said to them, "How is it you do not understand?" (Mark 8:17-21).

What was Jesus referring to here? And how could the leftover bread from the feeding of the 5,000 be a key to understanding the leaven of the Pharisees, the Sadducees and Herod? In Matthew 16:12, we are given more light on what leaven is: "Then they understood that He did not tell them to beware of the leaven of bread, but of the doctrine of the Pharisees and Sadducees." But if the leaven of the Pharisees and the Sadducees is merely their "doctrine," why was Herod lumped in with them? Again, what does their doctrine have to do with excess loaves of bread?

The answer may be in what leaven does: it "puffs up" the bread and makes it rise. With just a pinch, it exalts itself beyond measure. In 1 Corinthians 5:6, Paul says, "Your glorying is not good. Do you not know that a little leaven leavens the whole lump?" When Paul spoke of the work of leaven, it was in the context of a person's pride. In Luke 18:9-14, Jesus tells the following parable:

Two men went up to the temple to pray, one a Pharisee and the other a tax collector. The Pharisee stood and prayed thus with himself, "God, I thank You that I am not like other men—extortioners, unjust, adulterers, or even as this tax collector. I fast twice a week; I give tithes of all that I possess." And the tax collector, standing afar off, would not so much as raise his eyes to heaven, but beat his breast, saying, "God, be merciful to me a sinner!" I tell you, this man went down to his house justified rather than the other; for everyone who exalts himself will be humbled, and he who humbles himself will be exalted.

The self-righteous Pharisee prayed with head held high, puffing out his chest, thanking God that he wasn't like other men. It was pride that caused the Sadducees—the intellectual elite—to deny the existence of angels and the resurrection. And it was pride that caused Herod to murder John the Baptist rather than back down in front of his honored guests (see Matt. 14:1-12). Those who are proud are puffed up with a sense of their own carnal security. They are "high-minded," something that the Bible discourages us from being (see 1 Tim. 6:17). The proud, self-righteous man thinks that his own good works will save him. He is "puffed up" by his fleshly mind (see Col. 2:18).

In Luke 12:1, we are given further light on "leaven." Jesus said, "Beware of the leaven of the Pharisees, which is hypocrisy." Why is a man proud, why is he self-righteous, and why does he live in hypocrisy? Simply because he has not been humbled by the Law of God. He has never been brought low by the perfect Law of Liberty:

For if any be a hearer of the word, and not a doer, he is like unto a man beholding his natural face in a glass: For he beholds himself, and goes his way, and straightway forgets what manner of man he was. But whoso looks into the perfect law of liberty, and continues therein, he being not a forgetful hearer, but a doer of the work, this man shall be blessed in his deed (Jas. 1:23-25).

We have millions of people within the contemporary Church who have never been humbled by the Law so that they can see their sin. If you probe a little, you will find that they think they are good people. But when Jesus said, "Blessed are the poor in spirit, for theirs is the kingdom of heaven" (Matt. 5:3), He used a specific word for the word "poor." It is translated from *ptochos*, which literally means "to crouch or cower as one helpless." It signifies a beggar or a pauper. It refers to someone who is in abject poverty, totally dependent on others for help and destitute of even the necessities of life. That's our state, morally speaking, before a holy God. The Law shows us our state.

Yet multitudes sit in the midst of God's people as strangers to the spiritual nature of the Law and strangers to biblical repentance, thinking that they are saved when they are not. According to a 2007 study by The Barna Group, 26 percent of born-again Christians agree that "while He lived on earth, Jesus committed sins, like other people," compared to 41 percent of all adults. Thirty-seven percent of born-again Christians believe that if a person is good enough, he or she can earn a place in heaven.[5]

How can someone be converted to Christ when he or she believes that the Bible is wrong when it says that Jesus was without sin? How can that person understand the sacrifice of the cross if he or she thinks it was tainted by sin? How can someone believe that he or she is a good person when Jesus said there is none good but God (see Mark 10:18)? As Bill Bright once said, something is radically wrong.

DON'T GET BURNED

The firefighter doesn't want to get burned, so he wears multiple layers of protective clothing. Because his flesh is extremely vulnerable, he instinctively guards it from exposure to fire, which could cause him great pain. The Christian must be careful not to get burned by sin, particularly sexual sin. He knows that his flesh (his sinful Adamic nature) is extremely vulnerable. So he must put on layers of protection. If he doesn't, sin will eventually bring him great pain.

The Scriptures warn us to "flee sexual immorality" (1 Cor. 6:18). If King David had cut lust off at the eye level when he desired his neighbor's wife, it would have saved him a great deal of pain. He experienced the reality of lust bringing forth sin, and sin, when it is finished, brings forth death. The Christian knows that if his eye causes him to sin, it would be better for him to pluck it out and cast it from him rather than be cast into hell with both eyes (see Matt. 18:9).

Perhaps the most effective layer of protection for the Christian from the fires of lust is a deep gratitude for the cross. The Christian looks on the suffering Savior and sees the terrible cost that Jesus went to for his forgiveness. And in the light of it, he crucifies himself to the lust of the flesh, the lust of the eyes and the pride of life.

Lust is truly like a fire. The more you feed it, the bigger it gets, until it finally consumes you. In the movie *Fireproof*, lust almost consumed Caleb Holt. He eventually took a baseball bat and smashed his computer.[3] But you don't really need to do that. It was dramatic in the film, but you can't go through life breaking everything that tempts you to sin. If you can't handle the temptation, simply remove the computer from your home. Or better yet, cultivate the fear of the Lord in your heart so that the problem is dealt with at the most basic level. The Bible says, "Keep your heart with all diligence, for out of it springs the issues of life" (Prov. 4:23).

Remember that God sees everything. There is nothing that is hidden from His sight. So whatever else you do, deal with lust you must, or you will eventually get burned—both in this life and in the next.

—Kirk Cameron

Over the Edge

Some years ago, a friend flew me and my son-in-law to Israel. After visiting Jericho, we boarded a bus and made our way back through the mountainous passes toward Jerusalem. I was sitting right up front on the right side of a large bus while the rest of the group sat more toward the back.

The road was very narrow, with a deep valley on the right-hand side. As we approached a sharp left turn in the road, the driver slowed down, moved toward the right of the road and swung the steering wheel around the corner. The result was that my part of the bus went right over the edge of the road as we slowly turned. It was just then that I made the mistake of looking out of the window. *To my horror, I saw a 3,000-foot drop into the deep valley below.* For about two seconds I was sure that I was going to die. I was a dead man. Life was over. I was like a man who sees the smoke of a gun as it goes off and the bullet is two feet in front of his face. The experience was so real that it took my breath away.

Suddenly, the driver straightened the wheel. It was all over, and we were merrily driving along the road. The rest of the passengers were laughing and chatting, totally oblivious to what I had just experienced. I sat there in disbelief, almost in tears, and humbly thanked God that I was still alive. In a matter of two seconds, I had gained a new appreciation for my precious life. Even at this moment, I still benefit profoundly from that terrifying experience. I am forever thankful for the gift of life, and my gratitude is directed to God alone.

The moral Law hangs us over eternity. For those of us who experience true conviction of sin, it is an overwhelming horror. The reality of our depravity demands that we be damned forever. We look around at the rest of humanity and see that they are oblivious to what is happening. Life is a joyride, and death and damnation are far from their thoughts. But for us, the Law calls for our execution. It stirs a conscience that points its finger at our guilt. We are going to be damned, and there's no hope. None. The experience takes our breath away. Like the psalmist, we say, "My iniquities have overtaken me, so that I am not able to look up; they are more than the hairs of my head; therefore my heart fails me. Be pleased, O Lord, to deliver me; O Lord, make haste to help me!" (Ps 40:12-13).

But then we hear of the cross—the glorious good news of the cross! Jesus Christ suffered and died in our place while we were yet sinners. We hear that God has turned a corner for humanity through the gospel. The Law drives us to Christ, where we find everlasting life. Oh, the relief of God's mercy! Oh, the unspeakable gratitude that suddenly comes from nowhere and explodes toward God for His kindness!

Without the terrors of the Law, the professed Christian drives along the path of life with no appreciation for what he has been given in the gospel. That's why so many within the Church can sit passively in the pew. They have never experienced the wrath of the Law, and so they don't have gratitude enough to even consider doing the will of the God they profess to love.

Our European agent, Jim McMaster, once sent me an email that had come to him after he had sent a man a copy of the book *Hell's Best Kept Secret*. Jim said that 26 years ago, as a boy of 18, the man had "said a prayer," and that since then he had always assumed he was a Christian despite living a life of habitual sin. After several emails, Jim and the man had a 40-minute conversation on the phone. Jim had never heard anyone in so much anguish. He prayed with the man and left him with the Lord. Two days later, Jim received another email from the man.

Below are extracts from the man's emails to Jim (used with permission). Watch for the gratitude that comes when mercy supersedes wrath:

The difference I am experiencing in these past few days is so evident and precious. I feel sensitive toward sin, and I hope to continue so for the rest of my life. I read the Word so much more now, and my prayers seem more meaningful than before. I was completely shocked that God reached down to me and convicted me of my sin. I knew for the first time in my life that even though I was a genuine, believing, well-meaning "Christian" believer, I had been a false convert for 26 years. For over four days, I experienced enormous conviction of my sins. I was terrified because of the real knowledge of my sinful state flooding in my mind and my heart that I was going to hell. I was even more terrified of facing God, not being able to do anything (twist His arm) or even beg to get saved from my sin. I couldn't even appeal to God—He wouldn't even look in my direction—my sin was in the way. That is definitely a hell. I now understand the cross and the work done on it by my Lord for me. I am so very, very grateful for the love He has for me. I can now boldly approach the throne of grace in Jesus' name, without a single sin staining me, and speak with God, and He will turn His head in my direction and listen to me because I am His own. My email cannot express my joy!

The Law Showcases Grace

We are to preach the Word, be instant in season and out of season and, like Nathan, "*convince, rebuke,* exhort, with all longsuffering and teaching" (2 Tim. 4:2, emphasis added). We are not to be afraid to take sinners over the edge of eternity, because we know how it will benefit them when they come to faith in Christ. We also know that without the Law, they may not even come to faith.

They will instead experience a false conversion and sit as tares among the wheat until they are sorted out on the Day of Judgment and cast into hell. It was Charles Spurgeon who warned:

> Lower the Law and you dim the light by which man perceives his guilt; this is a very serious loss to the sinner rather than a gain; for it lessens the likelihood of his conviction and conversion. I say you have deprived the gospel of its ablest auxiliary [its most powerful weapon] when you have set aside the Law. You have taken away from it the schoolmaster that is to bring men to Christ. . . . They will never accept grace till they tremble before a just and holy Law. Therefore the Law serves a most necessary purpose, and it must not be removed from its place.[6]

A. N. Martin said, "The moment God's Law ceases to be the most powerful factor in influencing the moral sensitivity of any individual or nation, there will be indifference to Divine wrath, and when indifference comes in it always brings in its train indifference to salvation." Take out the Law, and people will reject any thought of God being angry at sinners. That's why so many are offended at the thought of a God who would create hell. *And that's why they don't embrace the gospel like a dying man.* They don't see their danger. This is such an important point. If I haven't made it clear, please go back a few pages and read it again. Millions sit in the contemporary Church thinking that they are saved when they are not. This is such a terrible tragedy, and yet the remedy is so simple: go back to biblical evangelism. Do what Jesus did.

If you know your Bible, you will know that without the Law, Israel strayed into idolatry, then into sexual sin, and then came judgment. History shows us that they continually forsook the Law, created a god in their own image, and that their dumb idol didn't tell them that fornication was wrong. This is what happened when Moses was up on the mountain receiving the Ten Commandments from God. Israel created an idol—a golden calf. They then took their clothes off, and then came judgment.

That is exactly what has happened in America. The Law has been banned in the public place and neglected in the pulpit. So the nation has no knowledge of the holiness of God. They bow to an idol that has no moral dictate. So off have come the clothes.

Tell the Ever-New Old Story

It's clear from Scripture that a genuine convert is one who hears and "understands" (see Matt. 13:23). This is perhaps why Philip the evangelist asked the Ethiopian eunuch if he *understood* what he was reading (see Acts 8:30).

It would seem obvious that this understanding is not only a reference to sin but also to the gospel. This is perhaps why the enemy is able to snatch the good seed from the wayside hearer, as told in the parable of the sower. It's because he doesn't *understand* that it is the message of everlasting life, so he puts no value to it:

> When anyone hears the word of the kingdom, and does not understand it, then the wicked one comes and snatches away what was sown in his heart (Matt. 13:19).

My great desire is for sinners to *understand* the gospel and be saved. Recently, I have discovered something exciting that has helped many of the people to whom I have witnessed to *understand.* While I want to share it with you, I do so with a little hesitation, lest you think my confidence is in my own abilities rather than in the Spirit of God.

I believe that anything I preach is a dead letter unless God makes it alive. My words, methods, anecdotes, parables and phrases cannot save a soul. God alone saves the sinner, from the sowing to the reaping. However, I also believe that as a preacher of the gospel, my job is to strive (with the help of God) to bring about understanding. And so, I use "great plainness of speech." I don't use "enticing words of man's wisdom." I keep the message simple in the hope that the sinner will grasp what I am trying to say.

So, my gospel presentation may begin with a parable about a man stealing another man's lamb (as with Nathan and David), or by quoting Athenian poets, as Paul did when he preached in Athens. I may use metaphors, similes, statistics, quotes, parables, personal experiences and, of course, I present the Law, the gospel and the necessity of repentance and faith.

I may equate repentance to a criminal who becomes law-abiding and shows his sincerity by returning stolen goods. Perhaps I will explain saving faith by differentiating it from an intellectual belief and likening it to *trusting* in a pilot or a parachute. I speak of the cross by explaining that it's like a civil judge paying a criminal's fine, thus satisfying the law and at the same time extending mercy. All these examples are aimed at (with the help of God) bringing *understanding* to the sinner. If the sinner doesn't understand the gospel, he or she won't value it and seek the Savior.

Now to the point. I want to explain to you why I think that I have seen more sinners surrender to Christ (in my personal witnessing) in the last 6 months than in the last 35 years.

Incorporating the Law into the gospel presentation does many things. It primarily shows sinners that they are criminals and that God is their judge. The Law (in the hand of the Holy Spirit) stops their mouth and leaves them guilty before God (see Rom. 3:19-20). It reveals that they deserve nothing but judgment for their crimes. Like a faithful prosecutor, the Law of God points its accusing finger, and so the sinners' stirred conscience bears witness and also points its finger at the criminal (see Rom. 2:15). The verdict is "guilty," and the condemnation is just. This is the scenario I try to paint for sinners. I do my best to put them in the courtroom on the Day of Judgment, with the hope that they will understand the mercy that God offers him in Christ.

For years when I did this, I then said, "You broke God's Law, and Jesus paid your fine in His life's blood." But early in 2008, I added the words, "It was a *legal* transaction. You broke God's Law (the Ten Commandments), and Jesus paid your fine. That means that God can *legally* dismiss your case. You can leave the courtroom on the Day of Judgment because another paid your fine. *Does that make sense?*" From the first time I said those words, I noticed again and again the light go on in the eyes of my listeners.

While those words are certainly not magic or formulaic, many people suddenly understood what I was saying when I explained the gospel that way. I can't point to a Bible verse that uses this exact language, but I can say that *legality* is the essence of the cross. It was God's love for justice *and* for guilty sinners that drove Him to Calvary. God is the "habitation of Justice" (Jer. 21:33). We are guilty criminals. The fine has been paid, and we can leave the courtroom.

Carefully explaining the gospel message by using legal vernacular when speaking to those whose understanding is "darkened" can sometimes give new light on what he or she perceives to be just an old and irrelevant story.

THE QUICKSAND
OF MORAL
RELATIVITY

I've written at length about how people do not understand the nature of sin and why their claims to "goodness" accrue nothing in the eyes of God. At the heart of this lack of understanding is the fact that they live in a world of moral relativity. It seems that a whole generation has lost a sense of what is right and what is wrong.[1]

While it can be argued that this is a way of thinking since sin entered the world, it can only enter when there is a moral vacuum, and that vacuum is a forsaking of God's Law. When the Law of God is completely upheld, there is no moral relativity. Morality becomes absolute. But when the Law is neglected, both in pulpits and in secular society, every man naturally becomes a law to himself because he has no other guide. He does what is right in his own eyes. He lives by his own standards rather than the standards of God.

This is why we have a generation that says, "What's right for you is right for you, and what's right for me is right for me." Studies indicate that 75 percent of American college professors currently teach that there is no such thing as right and wrong.[2] Rather, they treat the questions of good and evil as relative to "individual values and cultural diversity." Life becomes like an abstract painting, painted by a painter who painted with no intent. Of course, this makes no sense to the Christian, but it does to a spiritually blind world. They see it as tolerance in action. It's a "live and let live" coexistence.

But there is more to this than meets the eye. The moral relativist usually chooses to have no boundaries, because that leaves him to exercise what he believes is moral freedom. He is like a man who leaps from a cliff believing that he can fly until he finds that there is an absolute law that he neglected to bring into the equation: gravity. It brings all of us back to earth eventually.

The sinner leaps into sin with a reckless abandonment and experiences the elation of the pleasures of its fleeting joy. But the sinner will eventually find that there is an absolute Law that will bring him or her back down to earth and damn him or her for eternity.

Would You Shoot?

Let's test the boundaries of the philosophy of moral relativism. It's 1938. You have a high-powered telescopic weapon in your hands. Adolf Hitler is in your sights. You have one shot. Keep in mind the future of Nazi Germany. Do you take him out?

I often ask this question when I am witnessing. If people say they wouldn't shoot, I say, "Just one squeeze of your finger will save the lives of 6 million innocent Jews. These are mothers and fathers and their precious children. One squeeze will save them. In fact, the total estimated human loss of life caused by World War II was roughly 72 million people, making it the deadliest and most destructive war in human history. You could stop that massive tragic loss of precious human life. The civilian toll was around 47 million, including 20 million deaths due to war-related famine and disease. The military toll was about 25 million, including the deaths of about 4 million prisoners of war in captivity. The Allies lost approximately 61 million people, and the Axis powers lost 11 million. You could save them all with just one squeeze of your finger."

How about you? Would you take Hitler out? If you say that you wouldn't, how about if war had been declared and you had been enlisted in the military? Do you do your duty as a soldier and squeeze the trigger? If you don't carry out your military responsibility, you would be esteemed in the sight of Nazi Germany. They would give you a medal for not shooting der Führer. Imagine if a German soldier had Winston Churchill in his sights in 1942, but for some reason he didn't shoot. We would want to pat him on the back and give him a medal for helping our cause. Don't shoot, and you are a Nazi hero.

As you look through the lens of these "what if" scenarios and wonder what is morally correct, think of the little Jewish children. Look into their fear-filled eyes as they are stripped naked along with their parents and marched into deadly gas chambers. Think of the doctors extracting gold from the teeth of dead Jews, just before they are tossed into the ovens. Think of the workers who will make lampshades from the flesh of the murdered innocents.

Or are you a pacifist? If a man was going to rape and kill your mother and you had a gun in your hand, would you protect her? Or would you leave it up to God to make that call and believe for a miracle? How about your children? The Bible says, "But if any provide not for his own, and especially for those of his household, he has denied the faith and is worse than an unbeliever" (1 Tim. 5:8). Does that include protection? I wouldn't hesitate to pull the trigger. I would start at his foot and work my way up.

But let's say you are struggling with the Hitler issue, and then you say that you would shoot to save the lives of millions. You figure that even if God did damn you for taking Hitler's life, you have taken the high road and neglected your fate because you were thinking of the fate of others. Let's see where the high road leads.

Taking the High Road

It's 40 years earlier. You have Hitler's *mother* in your sights. She's pregnant with Adolf. You only have one shot. With the squeeze of your finger, do you take her out? One small squeeze? You would save more than 70 million human beings.

Most people say that they wouldn't. When I ask if their answer has anything to do with God, they usually say that it does. What would you do? If you say that you would take the high road and think of the fate of those millions rather than yourself, I have another question for you.

It's 1977. You have Jeffrey Dahmer in your sights. Dahmer murdered 17 men and boys between 1978 and 1991, most of whom were of African or Asian descent, with the majority of the murders occurring between 1987 and 1991. His murders were extremely gruesome, involving rape, torture, dismemberment, necrophilia and cannibalism. This man murdered and ate human beings. *He was more evil than Hitler.* Do you take him out? Think of the terrible suffering you will save. Think of the victims. Think of the horror the mothers and fathers and brothers and sisters of those poor victims will have to live with if you don't squeeze the trigger. If you say that you would kill him, I have one more moral dilemma for you.

Remember that during the 10-year period from 1997 to 2007, approximately 180,000 people were murdered in the United States. If you had each of those potential murderers in your sights before they committed the crime, would you pull the trigger? How about vicious rapists? So the question becomes, "Where do you stop pulling the trigger?"

The good news is that most of us will never have to face such perplexing dilemmas. But pondering them does make us think of where the moral boundaries lie. The Christian should attempt to determine that boundary by trying to seriously ascertain God's will in each one. If we are asked to pull the plug on a loved one because he or she is suffering, or give permission to take the life of a baby because we are told by doctors that it will be born without a brain, we will only do so in the light of the smile or the frown of God. That decision should be made in the light of holy Scripture, godly counsel and the fear of God.

But the moral relativist doesn't bother to bring God into the equation. He lives by what he or she feels or by what contemporary society dictates is right or wrong, whether the subject is euthanasia, abortion, homosexuality and so on.

So how does secular society carve out its morality? The usual explanation is that anything is morally acceptable as long as it doesn't harm another human being. To the secular world, evil is horizontal rather than vertical. Blasphemy is okay, because it doesn't hurt another human being. Abortion is okay because the fetus is not a human being, so murder is committed for the good of the mother. Fornication is okay. Homosexuality is okay. Adultery may even be said to help a marriage. Lying and even theft can easily be justified. So the moral Law is violated with no fear of consequence. The sinner jumps into sin with reckless abandon.

This is why the moral Law must be used to stir sinners' consciences. It shows sinners that they forgot to bring God into the equation, and that their evil is first of all vertical. Their every sin is against God and His Law. The Ten Commandments, like a faithful lighthouse, show sinners that their worldview is sending them toward sharp and dangerous rocks. It reveals that God sees their hatred as murder and that their burning lust had made them a serial rapist at heart. So when sinners are faced with what we call moral dilemmas, if they are going to pull the trigger on evil and be consistent, they have to turn the gun on themselves. That's where Calvary comes in.

IT MAY
TAKE TIME

One of the highlights of my life was to teach my kids about this world. There was a time when I explained why a bird sings, why the sky was blue, why the sun exists . . . yet in this age of knowledge, it wasn't long until my kids sped past me and began explaining life to me. Still, there are a few things that my boys (who are now married) can learn from me.

Take, for example, how I got out of having to weed the garden for a lifetime. This happened because I once kneeled down next to Sue and pulled out what I thought were weeds. They were her prized plants. She hasn't let me weed the garden for years. I haven't mowed the lawn for years either. This is because I thought that it would be a good idea to mow the entire lawn using a circular method. It sure was fast, but it looked so bad that we now have a gardener, who I am pleased to say (for a mere pittance) mows the lawn and weeds the garden. Both incidents were disasters at the time, but now that I look back, they sure worked out for my good.

The Bible takes this one step further. It tells us that whatever disasters come our way, God will definitely work things out for our good—if we love Him and we are called to His purposes (see

Rom. 8:28). This "good" may be evident immediately, it may take years, or it may not even happen in our lifetime. But if we fulfill our part, we can be sure that God will fulfill His. He is faithful to every promise He has made.

Let me tell you how God took 20 years to show His hand in something that slowly became a big-time disaster in my life.

The Battle

In 1989, my family and I were flown from New Zealand to Southern California, because a pastor from a certain denomination had heard me teach about "Hell's Best Kept Secret" and said, "America *must* hear this teaching." In 1990, another pastor took me to hear the denomination's evangelist. Afterward, he took me up to the pulpit, and just before he was about to introduce me, he put my book *Hell's Best Kept Secret* onto the pulpit. The evangelist looked at it and then said, "That guy *hates* [a certain well-known evangelist]." I could hardly believe what I had just heard. I *loved* the man. I mumbled, "No, he doesn't!"

The only way I could figure why he would say such a thing was that I had quoted statistics of the fall-away rate of the converts at his crusades and said that no doubt he and other well-known evangelists would be deeply concerned by such tragic figures. In retrospect, I should have left the issue nameless. Suddenly, we were back in our seats, dumbfounded at what we had just heard. But we quickly forgot about the incident.

As doors opened for our ministry throughout the United States, they remained closed in the larger churches of my own denomination. At one point, we obtained permission to have a book table at the yearly pastor's conference, but a week before the conference, they suddenly said there was no room for our table.

Students at the denomination's large Bible school told us that their principal had said, "I will go to be with the Lord before Ray Comfort speaks at this school." Not long after that, someone sent me a recording about false teachers, and within a minute of mentioning them, I was named. Then I heard rumors about me being a legalist and of my so-called hatred of the well-known evangelist. My pastor was even ostracized because I went to his church, and then I heard that my books had been banned from the denomination's bookstores.

While many smaller churches welcomed me, the bigwigs had made it plain that I wasn't at all welcome. Any reputation I had was shattered. I was known as a legalist—a false teacher who hated a famous evangelist. I sent the principal of the Bible school a $100 gift basket saying that I appreciated him and his love for God's Word, and after nearly 20 years of being part of a wonderful denomination, I felt that it was best that I leave.

The Change

Then something wonderful happened. A young pastor contacted me and told me that he had been "warned" about my ministry. However, he had taken the time to cautiously read *The Way of the Master* and had been blown away by the teaching. God did such a radical work in his life that he began open-air preaching with me each week.

Through some strange circumstances, this pastor had found himself as the youth evangelist and was meeting every week with the senior pastor of the entire denomination of 1,000 churches. Over the following months, he gently shared with the senior pastor how excited he was about my ministry. Then he arranged for me to have lunch with the principal of the Bible school. Despite it being a little nerve-wracking, four of us had a lunch that went down well. There was no contention.

A few weeks later, the Bible school principal was on a radio program when a caller asked what he thought of our ministry. He said that he had just had lunch with me and that I was the real deal. The caller said that she was pleased to hear that, because God saved her through our ministry.

A short time later, the youth pastor asked if he could have me speak at a conference at the main church in Southern California. To my surprise, that was cautiously okayed, as long as there were other speakers—"to bring a balance." Then, two days before the event, the youth evangelist asked if I could be a guest on the senior pastor's national radio program for 10 minutes to talk about the conference. Amazingly, that was also okayed. However, the day before I was due to go on air, he was sent an email from a pastor who was deeply distressed that I was not only going to be a speaker at a conference at the main church but also that I was appearing on the radio program. Fortunately, the email was ignored and the invitation was still on.

As I sat down with the host, the senior pastor walked into the studio, and then in came the principal of the Bible school. Suddenly, I was LIVE on "The Pastor's Perspective," and instead of giving me 10 minutes, they kept me for an hour answering theological questions from listeners around the country.

I could hardly believe what was happening. Think of it: I was the false Bible teacher who supposedly hated a certain famous evangelist and whose books were banned. I was supposedly so off in my teaching that the principal of the Bible School said that he would die before I would be invited to speak, and here I was answering theological questions on their national radio program.

FELLOWSHIP

Firefighters need each other. They can't afford to allow rifts to come between friendships. There is too much at stake. Their calling has to be a higher calling that supersedes petty disagreement. If two enter a fire, the creed is that two come out of the fire. They need unity of purpose. They strive to look out for the safety of their fellow firefighter.

As Christians, we have a calling that is too high for petty disagreements. We are to "stand fast in one spirit, with one mind striving together for the faith of the gospel" (Phil. 1:27). Think of what God asks us to do—to pull sinners from the fires of an eternal hell. How could we ever let anything take our eyes off that goal?

Jesus sent His disciples out in twos. There's good reason for this. You get to know your partner and what he can handle. Ray Comfort and I are not only ministry partners and friends, but we often preach and witness together. We have even helped each other pass out tracts.

I remember entering a bus in Chicago and sitting at the back. As Ray was walking down the aisle toward me, I said, "Hey, what are those in your pocket?" Immediately, everyone's eyes were looking at a stack of million-dollar bill tracts. He said, "Million-dollar bills. Did you folks get one?"

The passengers were suddenly holding out their hands and were thrilled to get their own million-dollar bill tract. That was just a small thing, but think of the implications if just one of those people read the message on the back of the tract and found everlasting life.

Other times, you may be called to watch your partner's back. When the flames of backbiting or gossip appear, learn to put them out with a gentle but thoroughly wet blanket. Some people have the gift of discouragement. Be on guard for them. They usually approach you with what they think is good advice. But it can be poison wrapped in candy, and it can get into your system. That's why you need a partner who will faithfully stand with you when the heat comes on. You need someone who will have nothing but encouragement for you.

—Kirk Cameron

More than 1,000 people showed up for the conference, and there were nothing but positive comments. How kind God is to take a disastrous and hopeless situation and work it out for my good and for the furtherance of His kingdom.

Get Ready

There is a strong possibility that if you attempt to get biblical evangelism into your church, you will also encounter some opposition. So, in the remainder of this chapter, I want to present some of the questions and objections that people have raised to the teaching and my response to each. In this way, I hope to give you some ideas for how you can anticipate some of the issues you may be faced with and how you can respond.

Do you believe that this method is always (or normally) used in the Bible? How often did the Lord and His apostles use this method?

Scripture is extremely consistent with the "Law to the proud and grace to the humble" principle. God resists the proud—always. The following are some examples:

- Mark 10:17-19: The Law was given to the rich young ruler.
- John 3:1-5: Grace was given to Nicodemus, the humble leader of the Jews.
- John 4:1-18: Jesus made reference to the Law in His discussion with the woman at the well, saying that she had violated the seventh commandment.
- Romans 2:21-24: Paul openly quoted the Ten Commandments.
- Acts 2:1-40: Peter preached at Pentecost, and his message was primarily grace because he was preaching to devout Jews who knew the Law.
- Acts 8:26-40: The eunuch was humble, and was therefore given grace.

• Acts 10:30-48: Again, the hearers were humble. They were therefore given grace.

Paul also used the Law when he spoke to the leaders of the Jews in Rome in Acts 28:23: "So when they had appointed him a day, many came to him at his lodging, to whom he explained and solemnly testified of the kingdom of God, persuading them concerning Jesus from both the Law of Moses and the Prophets, from morning till evening."[1]

Is there anywhere in Scripture where you find the Lord Jesus or His disciples using the Law on Gentiles in evangelism?

It is true that you will not find any examples in Scripture of the Lord Jesus evangelizing Gentiles using the Law. But neither did He evangelize any Gentiles using the message of grace. Remember that He said, "I was not sent except to the lost sheep of the house of Israel" (Matt. 15:24). His ministry was to the Jews, not to the Gentiles. A failure to understand the biblical principle of "Law to the proud and grace to the humble"—that God *resists* the proud—will leave us in confusion about why Jesus used the Law on some to whom He spoke and gave grace to others (see Mark 10:17; Luke 10:26; John 3:3-16).

In fact, it isn't until Acts 10 that we find the gospel being taken to the Gentiles, when a centurion named Cornelius receives a vision from the Lord and is told to seek out Peter. Cornelius and those at his house were humble of heart, so they were given the grace of God. However, when Paul preached Christ to the proud, he "explained and solemnly testified of the kingdom of God, persuading them concerning Jesus *from both the Law of Moses* and the Prophets, from morning till evening" (Acts 28:23, emphasis added).

In Romans 3:19, Paul says, "Now we know that whatever the law says, it says to those who are under the law, that *every* mouth may be stopped, and *all the world* may become guilty before God" (emphasis added). The Law was given to stop *every* mouth and leave the *whole world* (that's Jew *and* Gentile) guilty before God.

Does anyone in the Bible preach the gospel by saying that Christ has paid the debt for us?[2]

In John 19:30, we read that just before Jesus died on the cross, He said, "It is finished!" This is an accounting term, meaning that the debt had been paid in full. In Greek, the phrase is one word, *tetelestai*. In the ancient Greek world, when a debt was paid in full, the world *tetelestai* was written on the papyri texts that were used as receipts for taxes. This meant that the debt was totally paid.

The moral Law demanded payment for sin, and justice was fully satisfied with payment through the blood shed by Jesus on the cross. Because of the cross, God could then "be just and the justifier of the one who has faith in Jesus" (Rom. 3:26). It was Charles Spurgeon who said, "Until men know the law, their crimes have at least a palliation of partial ignorance, but when the code of rules is spread before them, their offenses become greater, since they are committed against light and knowledge. He who sins against conscience shall be condemned; of how much sorer punishment shall he be thought worthy who despises the voice of Jehovah, defies his sacred sovereignty, and willfully tramples on his commands. The more light the greater guilt—the law affords that light, and so causes us to become double offenders."[3]

Is it right to draw into question people's conversions just because they didn't use the Law?

I do not believe that a person's conversion should be questioned if the Law was not presented to him or her. Rather, I believe that if a person did not come through the doorway of repentance and faith, he or she cannot be saved. Some people have already been schooled by the Law and already recognize that they are sinners. They are already broken and humble. They need to be given grace. But for those who are proud and have not acknowledged their sinfulness, they need to be awakened to their sinfulness so that they realize what it is they need to repent of.

As ministers of the gospel, we have an obligation to tell our hearers to "examine [themselves] as to whether [they] are in the faith" (2 Cor. 13:5). Jesus warned that *many* would cry, "Lord, Lord," but not enter heaven, because they were workers of lawlessness (see Matt. 7:21,23). These are those who say they are Christians but they continue in *lawlessness*—they continue to violate God's Law (the Ten Commandments). I have received countless testimonies from people who thought they were saved, but once they understood the demands of the moral Law, they realized they were actually strangers to biblical repentance. Like Paul, they had not "known" sin without the Law, and so they didn't have the things that accompany salvation.

In December of 2008, researchers conducted a study of 30,000 high school students and found that 30 percent of students admitted to stealing from a store within the past year—a 2 percent rise from 2006. More than one-third of boys (35 percent) said that they had stolen goods, compared to 26 percent of girls. An overwhelming majority, 83 percent, of public school and private religious school students admitted to lying to their parents about something significant, compared to 78 percent for those attending independent nonreligious schools. According to the researchers, "Despite these high levels of dishonesty, the respondents have a high self-image when it comes to ethics. A whopping 93 percent said they were satisfied with their personal ethics and character and 77 percent said that when it comes to doing what is right, [they are] better than most people [they] know."[4]

These are violations of *God's* Law—lying, stealing and dishonoring of parents. It's significant that the religious schools had higher rates of lawlessness and that self-righteousness among the students at these institutions was rampant. While experts and philosophers suggest a multitude of reasons as to why this is happening, it can be traced back to a lack of the fear of God. These students' concept of God doesn't include retribution for transgression of His Law. Idolatry is probably the hardest sin to detect, but it is undoubtedly the worst of them because of the doors it opens.

Other surveys reveal that 62 percent of Americans say that they have a relationship with Jesus Christ that is "meaningful to them." But 91 percent lie regularly, and 37 percent of born-again (Christians) believe that if a person is good enough, they can earn a place in heaven.[5] Eighteen percent of all abortions are performed on women who identify themselves as "born-again/evangelical"; just under one in five of those who murder their own children in the womb profess to love the Lord.[6] These statistics should alarm us and confirm the words of Jesus that the Church is filled with tares among the wheat (see Matt. 13:24-30).

I am as obligated to warn those who sit within the Church but lack fruit to confirm their salvation (see Matt. 7:18) as much as I am to warn the unsaved who are outside of the Church. We need to also ask the question as to why so many false converts are filling the Church. I believe that it's because of an unbiblical presentation of the gospel.

If using the Law on Gentiles were so important, wouldn't we see at least one example of this in the epistles?

Actually, we *do* see examples of this in the epistles. Look at Paul's words in Romans: "You, therefore, who teach another, do you not teach yourself? You who preach that a man should not steal, do you steal [the eighth commandment]? You who say, 'Do not commit adultery,' do you commit adultery [the seventh commandment]? You who abhor idols, do you rob temples [the first and second commandments]? You who make your boast in the law, do you dishonor God through breaking the law? For 'the name of God is blasphemed among the Gentiles because of you,' [referring to the third commandment] as it is written" (2:21-24).

It is true that the Law reveals sin, but don't the Gentiles already have the work of the Law in their hearts and the Holy Spirit convicting them?

In 1 Timothy 1:8-9, Paul states, "But we know that the law is good if one uses it lawfully, knowing this: that the law is not made for a righteous person, but for the lawless and insubordinate, for the ungodly and for sinners." The context of Paul's instruction to Timothy (the one he called an "evangelist"—see 2 Timothy 4:5) is brought out in verse 8. Paul says that the Law is good if it is used lawfully. He then says that the Law was made for the "lawless" and for "sinners." In verse 9, he points to specific lawless people: murderers (sixth commandment), those involved in sexual sin (seventh commandment) and liars (ninth commandment). Then in verse 11, he ties the context back into the gospel that was entrusted to him.

If the Law wasn't necessary because the Gentiles already had a knowledge of sin, why did Paul then say, "I would not have known sin *except through the law*" (Rom. 7:7, emphasis added)? Why didn't he say that he had a conscience and that was all he needed? But he maintained that it was the Law that gave him the knowledge of sin (see Rom. 3:20). Are Gentiles less sinful that Paul? Without the Law, Paul's understanding as to the exceedingly sinful nature of sin wouldn't have been known to him (see Rom. 7:13). Both Jew and Gentile need the Law, and Scripture says that's why God gave it (see Rom. 3:19-20).

Also, why would Paul have *reasoned* with Felix (the Roman procurator of Judea—a Gentile) about "righteousness, self-control, and the judgment to come" (Acts 24:25) if Felix already had a knowledge of sin through his conscience? Why, when he preached Christ, would he have used the Law of Moses in Acts 28:23 if his hearers already had the knowledge of sin?

The next time you share your faith, simply ask the person or persons to whom you are witnessing if they think that they are a good person. You will see the truth of Proverbs 20:6. They will almost certainly say that they are a good person, and they say this because they are ignorant of God's righteousness.

This is what Jesus did in Mark 10:17. He addressed the rich young ruler's ignorance about the meaning of the word "good."

Then He used the Law to bring the knowledge of sin—to show the young man *God's* standard of righteousness. That's what Jesus did when He evangelized—Law to the proud and grace to the humble. Why would we do anything different when we have been told to imitate Him?

How big is God in your message and in the work of convicting and drawing the sinner? Is He being replaced by method?

The Holy Spirit convicts of sin (which is transgression of the Law, see 1 John 3:4), righteousness (which is *of* the Law) and judgment (which is *by* the Law, see Rom. 2:12; Jas. 2:12). However, preaching is the method that God has chosen to use to reach the lost. If people are saved entirely by the Holy Spirit without preaching, then why does Scripture say, "It pleased God through the foolishness of the message preached to save those who believe"? (1 Cor. 1:21) and, "How shall they hear without a preacher?" (Rom. 10:14). Failure to work with the Holy Spirit (by preaching biblical truth) will fill the Church with false converts. We already have millions in that category, because of an unbiblical gospel presentation.[7] Charles Spurgeon said:

> We tell men to repent and believe, not because we rely on any power in them to do so, for we know them to be dead in trespasses and sins; not because we depend upon any power in our earnestness or in our speech to make them do so, for we understand that our preaching is less than nothing apart from God; but because the gospel is the mysterious engine by which God converts the hearts of men, and we find that, if we speak in faith, God the Holy

Spirit operates with us, and while we bid the dry bones live, the Spirit makes them live—while we tell the lame man to stand on his feet, the mysterious energy makes his ankle-bones to receive strength—while we tell the impotent man to stretch out his hand, a divine power goes with the command, and the hand is stretched out and the man is restored. The power lies not in the sinner, not in the preacher, but in the Holy Spirit, who works effectually with the gospel by divine decree, so that where the truth is preached the elect of God are quickened by it, souls are saved, and God is glorified. Go on, my dear brethren, preaching the gospel boldly, and be not afraid of the result, for, however little may be your strength, and though your eloquence may be as nothing, yet God has promised to make his gospel the power to save, and so it shall be down to the world's end.[8]

Wouldn't adopting this approach expose people to legalism in the Church?

"Legalism" is usually defined as any attempt to rely on our own self-effort to either attain or maintain our justification before God. This is heresy. I believe in salvation by grace alone, through faith alone. I preach the love of God through the blood of the cross. Some may say that I am "dogmatic" or "adamant" in my beliefs, but I am always open to reason if a person can convince me from Scripture that I am wrong. In fact, I have had this conversation many times with many godly men, who have searched the Scriptures and come back convinced that what I teach is thoroughly biblical.

A Biblical Approach

In 1952, the late Bill Bright wrote a little booklet called "The Four Spiritual Laws" as a means of clearly summarizing the Christian message for the purpose of leading others to Christ. These four spiritual laws are: (1) God loves you and offers a wonderful plan for your life; (2) Man is sinful and is separated from God, and therefore cannot know and experience God's love and plan for his life; (3) Jesus Christ is God's only provision for man's sin, and (4) We must individually receive Jesus Christ as our Savior and Lord so that we can know and experience God's love and plan for our lives.[9] Today, this is likely the most widely distributed religious booklet in history, with approximately 2.5 billion in print.[10]

What is interesting is that a year before Dr. Bright died, Kirk Cameron and I had breakfast at his house. During our conversation, he acknowledged that he had left out some very important issues in his presentation to the lost. He said, "I have thus come to see that silence, or even benign neglect on these subjects, is disobedience on my part. To be silent on the eternal destinations of souls is to be like a sentry failing to warn his fellow soldiers of impending attack."[11] The fact that he was willing to acknowledge such things is another testimony to the amazing character of this very godly man.

As you begin to conquer your fear and share your faith, you will undoubtedly be confronted with people who do not like your approach or who disagree with the methods you are using to share the gospel of Christ. Expect this opposition and be open to listening to what people have to say, but know that presenting the Law to people in order to get them to realize they are sinners and not being silent on the issue of "the eternal destinations of souls" is a completely biblical approach.

GOD CAN USE
SOMEONE ELSE

I was sitting in an airport when a large woman tried to get by my bag to sit beside me. I apologized, moved my bag, and down she plunked. I heard her say, "Thanks a million," so I said, "Did you just say, 'Thanks a million?' Here's a million dollars for you." She burst out laughing and spent the next two minutes raving about the tract.

I said, "So you like the million. Let me show you how I make my money." I then did a little sleight-of-hand, and she loved that also. She was originally from the Bronx in New York and had a thick New York accent. Her name was "Roberta," and she kept saying, "You are such a nice man." She said it so many times that I asked if she was Jewish. Jewish moms tend to say things like that. She was.

I continued showing her love and kindness, and she kept saying that I was a nice man. I guessed that I would no longer be Mr. Nice Guy if I witnessed to her. But her salvation was way more important than my male ego, so after about 30 minutes of being nice, I asked her what she thought happens after someone dies. Here's how the conversation went:

"Are you a born-again Christian?" she asked.

"Yes, but 'born-again Christian' is a superfluous phrase. That's like saying I'm a medical doctor physician. If I'm born again, I'm a Christian. If I'm a Christian, I've been born again."

My theological lesson seemed to go over her head. She said, "I've been born again. I used to be a German guard in the World War II."

"You mean, you believe in reincarnation?"

"Yes. I was shot because I didn't like what was going on."

"Really?"

"Yes."

"I was also around at the time of Jesus. I was an Egyptian. I was buried in a tomb."

"So, Roberta, if there is a heaven, do you think you are good enough to go there? Are you a good person?"

"I'm a very good person."

"Well, I will ask you a few questions to see if that's true. We will look at the Law of Moses for a minute." I then proceeded to go through the list. She had told many lies in her life, she had stolen things, and she had also blasphemed and lusted. It was around that time I was thinking, *No more Mr. Nice Guy.*

"Based on what you've told me, would you be innocent or guilty?" I said.

"I would go to hell," she said. I could feel a slight offense in her tone, but she wasn't angry. "I don't believe in Jesus," she said. "I'm Jewish, my husband is Jewish, my children are Jewish, and I will never believe in Jesus."

I got the message. She was saying, "No further, buddy." So I thanked her for listening and we talked of other things. She said, "You're a nice man." She then told me that she was in Overeaters

Anonymous (why tell me that, if it was "anonymous"?) and that she believed in a Higher Power.

She needed extra time, so she said that she was going to board early. I told her that I hoped she had a safe flight (that was because I was on her flight). When I got on the flight, I saw her talking on her cell phone and found that she was in my row, one seat over. As I passed her, I heard her saying something about meeting a nice man. When I sat by her, she couldn't believe it. There were more than 100 seats on the plane, and I was one seat over from her. She kept on with the conversation, saying that the nice man was sitting right by her, and she couldn't believe it.

Think of it. I had told her that she was on her way to hell, and she still thought well of me.

Roberta was spilling over into the middle seat between us, and she was concerned for the person who was going to sit in that seat. I leaned over and said, "I will develop severe bad breath and get rid of him." She thought that was very funny. I should have kept my mouth shut, because the man that sat between us had *really* bad breath, and her pushing him over pushed his breath all over me. It was so bad that I was afraid he would breathe on my computer screen and cause it to shut down. When the airline gave me two earplugs, I was tempted to put them up my nose.

Just then a couple of friendly flight attendants stood in the aisle and asked for million dollar bill tracts. They were Christians who had seen *The Way of the Master* TV program and boldly said, "This is a blessed flight. We all love Jesus. This flight is covered in the blood."

That was good for Roberta to hear, but not so good for Mr. Bad Breath. My cover was blown. But instead of being offended, he asked, "So what are the millions?" I gasped, "Here's yours," but didn't follow it up with, "So, what do you think happens when someone dies?" I was afraid of dying myself if I was hit face-on with his breath.

He passed the bill to his wife who was (understandably) sitting in the row behind us. I then gave him a copy of "What Hollywood Believes" and prayed that God would speak to him through the CD so that I wouldn't have to. When he went to sleep, even with his mouth closed I was being blasted through his nostrils. He had an eye cover on, so I reached up and adjusted his air to redirect the flow. That didn't work. My last resort was to hope that he would open his mouth while he slept so that I could toss in a packet of peppermints.

Did I fail with Roberta? Definitely not. I was able to go through the Ten Commandments and give her literature and a CD. She told me one of her good friends was a "born again," so I prayed that God would continue to speak to her though her friend.

Did I fail with Mr. Bad Breath? Yep. But I have the consolation that God doesn't need me to speak to a sinner. He can always use someone else, for which I am extremely grateful. (Perhaps you will be the one God will use to speak to him.)

The Importance of a Name

On the flight back to Atlanta, I sat down in a window seat. Minutes later, a large man sat down in the aisle seat. He was huge and, like Roberta, unable to put the armrest down because of the size of his stomach. I said, "Good morning, sir. How are you?" He glanced at me and mumbled, "Hey."

His "hey" was very telling. It told me he hated Christians. It told me he definitely didn't want to talk. It revealed that this man was a bitter, angry, hate-filled human being who was so stressed with life that he was going to kill the next person who tried to ram religion down his godless throat.

I ignored my fears and asked, "What's your name? I'm Ray." He smiled slightly and told me that his name was Ron.

Make sure you get and remember a person's name. Think of someone you know who has the same name and picture that person in your mind to help lock it in your memory banks when you are asking yourself, "Was it Rob or Ron, Rick or Ralph, Eric or John?" This is important because you are aiming to ask him a personal question—"What do you think happens after someone dies?" It makes it so much easier to be able to say, *Ron, I* have a question for you. What do you think happens after someone dies?"

I have asked hundreds, if not thousands, of people if they would like to do a quick on-camera interview for television. I say, "Excuse me, sir. Would you like to do an interview for television?" Most will immediately say, "No, thanks," and just walk on. I guess my offer made them feel important, like a politician who says "no comment" to the prying media. Their rejection made me feel like a door-to-door salesman.

However, I formulated a way to get interviews. When I would see a man with a tattoo, wearing a black T-shirt and baseball hat or something else like that, I would say, "Excuse me, sir. I'm doing interviews with buff men who wear black T-shirts, wear baseball hats and have tattoos." That would always produce an immediate smile. Then I would ask, "What's your name?" The man would say, "Eric" or whatever his name was, and I would say, "Eric, my name is Ray. Can you give me two minutes for a quick interview?" If I got the name, I would get the interview. It again showed me how important it is to break the ice by finding out the person's name and locking it in my memory bank so that it could be withdrawn when needed.

It turned out that the man on the airplane, Ron, (or was it Rob?) was a very warm individual who was very concerned that someone was going to sit in the seat between us. After my last flight, I was too. I asked him what he did for a job, and then halfway through the flight, I said, "Ron, I have a question for you. What do you think happens after someone dies? Do you think there's a heaven? Do people get reincarnated?"

"No. I don't think they are reincarnated."

"Do you think there's a heaven?"

"Yes. And there's the other place."

"Do you think you will go to heaven? Are you a good person?"

"I hope I will go there."

"Well, there's a way to find out with four simple questions. How many lies have you told in your life?"

"Thousands."

Ron was open and friendly. He listened and nodded with every word I said. When I asked him if he had a Bible, he said he had three. I encouraged him to read one of them and gave him a copy of the booklet "Save Yourself Some Pain."

I was so pleased with the conversation that I didn't have time to listen to my fears. But what if things don't go according to plan? We will look at that in the next chapter.

SPEAKING TO INTELLECTUALS

Say that you are sitting on an airplane and you finally get up courage to speak to the man sitting next to you. As he sips his coffee, you say, "Hey, Brian, I have a question for you. What do you think happens after someone dies?" Brian finishes the last gulp of his coffee, thinks for a minute and says, "Nothing." You say, "Nothing?" He smiles condescendingly and says, "I'm an atheist." Now you are the one who gulps, and you are not finishing anything but your desire to end this conversation. This man is obviously an intellectual. He's a thinker. He probably has a university degree. What do you say now?

Here's what you need to do. Stop thinking that Brian is an "intellectual." That's just not true. There is a possibility that he has a high IQ, but he is not a deep thinker. He's a "fool" according to the Bible (see Ps. 14:1 and Rom. 1:22). He is very shallow in his thoughts. He is of the same mentality as a man who believes that no one made the airplane you are both sitting on. The seats, the wings, the lighting, the sound system, the on-board television and radio, the engines, the carpet, the intricate wiring—all of these things happened by accident. There was nothing. Then came a big bang, and (in time), an airplane appeared—from nothing. Such thoughts are bordering on insanity, or are at most thoughts from the mind of a simpleton.

So why do we insist on believing that atheists are intellectual? Why do so many universities pump out atheists like there is no tomorrow?

Jesus called our enemy "the father of lies." Do you believe Him? We are surrounded by lies. Anyone who studies the theory of Darwinian evolution without prejudice and without blind faith knows that it is a lie. Atheism is a lie. It is intellectual suicide. Anyone who uses his God-given brain to think knows this. But still the lie persists that both those who believe in a crazy theory called "evolution" and the insanity of atheism are somehow intellectual.

The Lie List[1]

It is no big deal to some atheists, who lie, exaggerate or embellish the truth—just a little—to strengthen their argument that there is no God. Numerous atheist websites list "great minds" who were atheists. These are impressive at first glance. The problem is that what they maintain about these men and women simply isn't true. Few in their long lists are actual atheists. Take, for instance, the following small list of big names given in a challenge by a man who regularly frequents my blog:

I find it funny to note that not one person has accepted my challenge to find "Great Americans" (citizens who made great contributions to America's treasured literature, science, engineering, and who orchestrated social reforms that made America great) who are "Evangelical

Fundamentalist Christians" . . . I've actually done research, and I know of at least three, and they are nothing of the caliber of great Americans like Thomas Edison, Mark Twain, Robert Frost, Ernest Hemingway and Susan B. Anthony (who are, incidentally, all atheists). . . . Why have so many great contributions to Americans and world society been made by atheists, and so few by Evangelicals? The challenge is still open.

Look at his impressive list of great American atheists: (1) Thomas Edison, (2) Mark Twain, (3) Robert Frost, (4) Ernest Hemingway, and (5) Susan B. Anthony. I wonder how many gullible theists have become atheists because they believe that so many great minds of history denied the existence of God? The problem is that only one person in the above list of five was an actual atheist, and his story is a very sad case indeed. Let's look one by one at these great Americans who were "all" atheists.

Thomas Edison

Thomas Alva Edison (1847-1931) was an American inventor and businessman who developed many devices that greatly influenced modern life, including the phonograph and the long-lasting and practical electric light bulb.

I recently devoured a biography about this incredible man to whom we owe so much. I am consoled by his statement, "I have not failed 700 times. I have not failed once. I have succeeded in proving that those 700 ways will not work." I love his philosophy of "I find out what the world needs. Then, I go ahead and invent it."

So, was Thomas a Doubting Thomas? Far from it. Like many thinking minds, he simply hated the hypocrisy of "religion."

However, Edison was *not* an atheist. In fact, he is reported to have said the following:

> I do not believe in the God of the theologians; but that there is a Supreme Intelligence I do not doubt.[2]

> I am much less interested in what is called God's word than in God's deeds. All Bibles are man-made.[3]

Henry Ford once said, "I believe God is managing affairs and that He doesn't need any advice from me. With God in charge, I believe everything will work out for the best in the end. So what is there to worry about." Ford was a very close friend of Edison, and after his death he said, "[Edison] felt there was a central processing core of life that went on and on. That was his conclusion. We talked of it many times together. . . . Call it religion or what you like, Mr. Edison believed that the universe was alive and that it was responsive to man's deep necessity. It was an intelligent and hopeful religion if there ever was one. Mr. Edison went away expecting light, not darkness."[4]

Mark Twain

Samuel Langhorne Clemens (1835-1910), better known by the pen name Mark Twain, was an American humorist, satirist, lecturer and writer. Twain, like Edison, had a disdain for the hypocrisy of established religion. However, also like Edison, he was definitely not an atheist, as the following statements from him attest:

> God puts something good and lovable in every man His hands create.[5]

No man that has ever lived has done a thing to please God—primarily. It was done to please himself, then God next.[6]

None of us can be as great as God, but any of us can be as good.[7]

Robert Frost

Robert Lee Frost (1874-1963) was an American poet. He is highly regarded for his realistic depictions of rural life and his command of American colloquial speech. He was honored frequently during his lifetime, receiving four Pulitzer Prizes. In a letter to his friend G.R. Elliot in 1947, Frost alluded to one of his very real fears: "My fear of God has settled down into a deep and inward fear that my best offering may not prove acceptable in his sight." In a letter to Louis Untermeyer in 1932, Frost stated that he feared the "God of Israel, who admits he is a jealous God." In his final letter, written a few days before he died, he stated, "Salvation we will never have from anyone but God."[8] As in the case of Thomas Edison and Mark Twain, Robert Lee Frost was not an atheist.

Susan B. Anthony

Susan Brownell Anthony (1820-1906) was a prominent, independent and well-educated American civil rights leader who, along with Elizabeth Cady Stanton, led the effort to secure women's suffrage in the United States. When on trial for her convictions, she defended herself by stating, "May it please your honor, I shall never pay a dollar of your unjust penalty. . . . And I shall earnestly and persistently continue to urge all women to the practical recognition of the old revolutionary maxim, that 'Resistance to tyranny is obedience to God.'"[9]

Once again, like Edison, Frost and Mark Twain, she didn't deny the existence of God. Look at her own words:

> I always distrust people who know so much about what God wants them to do to their fellows. I distrust those people who know so well what God wants them to do, because I notice it always coincides with their own desires.[10]

> The Declaration of Independence, the United States Constitution, the constitutions of the several States and the organic laws of the Territories, all alike propose to *protect* the people in the exercise of their God-given rights. Not one of them pretends to bestow rights: "All men are created equal, and endowed by their Creator with certain inalienable rights. Among these are life, liberty and the pursuit of happiness. To secure these, governments are instituted among men, deriving their just powers from the consent of the governed."[11]

She also said, "The preamble of the constitution of the State of New York declares the same purposes. It says: 'We the people of the State of New York, grateful to Almighty God for our freedom, in order to secure its blessings, do establish this constitution.' Here is not the slightest intimation either of receiving freedom from the United States Constitution, or of the State's conferring the blessings of liberty upon the people; and the same is true of every other State constitution. Each and all declare rights God-given, and that to secure the people in the enjoyment of their inalienable rights is their one and only object in ordaining and establishing government."[12]

Ernest Hemmingway

Ernest Miller Hemingway (1899-1961) was a novelist, short-story writer and journalist. He received the Pulitzer Prize in 1953 for *The Old Man and the Sea* and the Nobel Prize in Literature in 1954. He once said, "All thinking men are atheists," which makes me suspect that the atheist "lie-list" may not be something new.

Hemmingway, who fought in the First World War, perhaps revealed his own thoughts about God in one of his plays. A reviewer said the following of *A Farewell to Arms*:

> As a Lieutenant during World War I, Frederic Henry claims to have no religion or love for God. In a conversation with his group's priest, Frederic only admits to be fearful of God "in the night sometimes." The reason why he only feels this at night is because it is the loneliest time; the time when there is a chance to think about the terrible and meaningless war, as well his meaningless life.[13]

Ernest Hemingway was the only atheist in the list of five supposed great Americans atheists. The prolific writer's life is a sad testimony to the truth of the words of Jesus, where He describes a man who built his house on sand and, when the storms of life came, the house tragically crumbled:

> On a safari [Hemingway] was the victim of two successive plane crashes. The injuries he got away with were grave and numerous. He sprained his right shoulder, arm, and left leg, had a grave overall concussion, temporarily lost his vision in the left eye, his hearing in the left ear, had a paralysis of the sphincter, crushed his vertebra, suffered

from a ruptured liver, spleen and kidney and was marked by first degree burns on his face, arms and leg. As if this was not enough, he was badly injured one month later in a brushfire accident which left him with second degree burns on his legs, front torso, lips, left hand and right forearm. The physical pain caused him to lose his mind. His strength was gone entirely, and so was his will to live.[14]

When we don't build our lives on the teaching of Jesus, the storms of life will eventually cause our downfall. Sadly, Ernest Hemmingway turned to alcohol to try and drown his sorrows. He attempted suicide in the spring of 1961 and received treatment, but it was unable to prevent his suicide on July 2, 1961. At 5:00 A.M., he died from a self-inflicted shotgun blast to the head. God only knows what happened moments before he took his life.

Einstein and God

There are many people who, in an attempt to show atheism to be "intellectual," have claimed that Albert Einstein, another great intellectual thinker, was also an atheist. But is there any proof those these claims? Let's take a closer look at Einstein's life and his own words to see if we can determine the answer.

Albert Einstein was a reluctant celebrity. Wherever he went, the spotlight was on him, but he seemed to be mystified as to why the world was so fascinated by him. (Then again, it's kind of hard not to notice a man with a big white moustache and a stack of white hair that resembles a scarecrow in a high wind—and this in a day when most every man's hair was kept short.) Even many years after his death, we are still deeply interested in what made this colorful man tick.

Albert's clock started ticking on March 14, 1879, and stopped when he died on April 18, 1955. He was a German-born Jewish physicist who is best known for his theory of relativity and, specifically, the mass-energy equivalence, $E = mc^2$. In 1999, Einstein was named *Time* magazine's "Person of the Century," and a poll of prominent physicists named him the greatest physicist of all time. He had such an impact upon modern culture that the name "Einstein" has become synonymous with the word "genius."

So, what did this man believe about God and the Bible? The brilliant scientist once said the following about his own beliefs:

> In view of such harmony in the cosmos, which I, with my limited human mind, am able to recognize, there are yet people who say there is no God. But what really makes me angry is that they quote me for support of such views.[15]

Einstein was a theist. He believed in God, but he definitely wasn't a Christian, and he didn't believe the Bible was the Word of God. In fact, throughout his life he denied that God could be personal, and he (like most people nowadays) was especially offended by the thought that God would hold any person accountable for their sins. Here's what he said:

> We know nothing about [God and the world] at all. All our knowledge is but the knowledge of schoolchildren. Possibly we shall know a little more than we do now. But the real nature of things, that we shall never know, never.[16]

Yet despite Einstein's clinging to the god of his own creation, he couldn't help but notice the genius of the Creator, and here he reveals his knowledge of some Scripture:

I see a pattern, but my imagination cannot picture the maker of the pattern. I see a clock, but I cannot envision the clockmaker. The human mind is unable to conceive of the four dimensions, so how can it conceive of a God, before whom a thousand years and a thousand dimensions are as one.[17]

Again, although Einstein denied that God was personal, he did catch a glimpse of His amazing hand:

I'm not an atheist. I don't think I can call myself a pantheist. The problem involved is too vast for our limited minds. We are in the position of a little child entering a huge library filled with books in many languages. The child knows someone must have written those books. It does not know how. It does not understand the languages in which they are written. The child dimly suspects a mysterious order in the arrangement of the books but doesn't know what it is. That, it seems to me, is the attitude of even the most intelligent human being toward God. We see the universe marvelously arranged and obeying certain laws but only dimly understand these laws.[18]

"What separates me from most so-called atheists is a feeling of utter humility toward the unattainable secrets of the harmony of the cosmos," he explained. In fact, Einstein tended to be more critical of debunkers, who seemed to lack humility or a sense of awe, than of the faithful. "The fanatical atheists," he wrote in a letter, "are like slaves who are still feeling the weight of their chains which they have thrown off after a hard struggle. They are creatures who—in their grudge against traditional religion as the 'opium of the masses'—cannot hear the music of the spheres."[19]

When asked the question, "To what extent are you influenced by Christianity?" He said, "As a child I received instruction both in the Bible and in the Talmud. I am a Jew, but I am enthralled by the luminous figure of the Nazarene."[20] When asked if he accepted the historical existence of Jesus, he replied, "Unquestionably! No one can read the Gospels without feeling the actual presence of Jesus. His personality pulsates in every word. No myth is filled with such life."[21] Einstein also said, "I want to know how God created this world. I am not interested in this or that phenomenon, in the spectrum of this or that element. I want to know His thoughts. The rest are details."[22]

Those who take the time to read the Bible can know how God created this world (see Gen. 1), and they can read the thoughts of God throughout Holy Scripture. But the reason many won't believe it is because it's not merely a history book, it is a *moral* book, and for that reason sinful man refuses to accept its pages. The psalmist informs us that "the entrance of Your words gives light" (Ps. 119:130), and the Bible further tells us that men love darkness rather than light, because their deeds are evil. They refuse to come to the light because it exposes their sinful deeds (see John 3:19-20).

Faith and the Human Intellect

During World War II, Air Force records revealed that a plane and her crew had completely disappeared on their first combat mission. The aircraft was found an incredible 1,000 miles past its target. Investigators found that the crew had bailed out of the plane just before it crashed in the 140-degree heat of the Libyan Desert.

STAY SHARP

The firefighter must keep his ax sharp and his arm strong. The time may come when someone's life depends on the edge of the ax and the strength of his arm.

The Christian has access to what Charles Spurgeon called "our ablest auxiliary." By that he meant our most powerful weapon. He was referring to the Law of God. It is the Law that effectively breaks down barriers and brings the endangered victim to the safety of the cross.

We especially need to be prepared when dealing with "intellectuals." The person may hold up the theory of evolution, the issue of suffering or other issues that will hinder his salvation. So the Christian must take the ax of the moral Law and destroy those barriers.

The Christian must make straight the way of the Lord. Every valley must be filled and every mountain removed.

The Christian does this by putting his energies toward the sinner's conscience.

How do we keep our ax sharp and our arm strong? By going through the Law again and again until it's second nature to us. Each time we witness is a workout, and we will get stronger each time we share our faith.

The Law is also like a 10-rung ladder. It enables us to reach those who are perishing by speaking to the heart of the issue. The "work of the Law" is written on the heart, and it shows sinners their danger. It lets them smell the smoke of the fires of a terrible hell so that they will respond with open arms to the gospel.

—Kirk Cameron

The bodies of most of the crew were discovered 78 miles from where they bailed out. One of the men had walked 114 miles before he died. What baffled military experts for years was how any plane could end up 1,000 miles past its target.

This is what happened: A strong back wind had caused them to arrive at their destination faster than the time they had estimated. Their instruments told them they had arrived, but they made the fatal mistake of not believing their instruments and instead trusting their own natural senses. Those who rely on their own human intellect make the same fatal mistake when it comes to their eternal salvation. As the Scripture states, "Trust in the LORD with all your heart, and lean not on your own understanding; in all your ways acknowledge Him, and He shall direct your paths" (Prov. 3:5-6).

Many years ago, I ran a kid's club. At the conclusion of our time together, I would take out a huge bag and give each child a piece of candy. One day as I told the kids to line up, I saw that the little brat bullies had pushed their way to the front. At the back were the meek, quiet, sickly kids. I remember thinking, *That is a line of greed if I ever I saw one.* But then I had an idea. I said, "Kids, stay right where you are. Everybody turn about-face. If you move out of line, you're not getting any candy." Every kid turned about-face, and I had great delight in taking that big bag of candy to the other end of the line and giving it first to those meek, quiet, sickly kids—much to the disgust of the greedy brats at the back.

That's how God has trapped the wicked in their own craftiness. He has turned the line around. In this world where the rich get richer and the poor get stomped on, God has done something incredible: He resists the proud but gives grace to the humble (see Prov. 3:34). Ask a proud person if he or she admits to being a sinner, deserves nothing but hell, and is willing to repent and follow Jesus Christ no matter what the cost and you will usually hear, "Of course not! I don't believe that silly message!" Behold the wisdom and infinite intelligence of God. The Bible says He's chosen the foolish things of the world to confound the wise (see 1 Cor. 1:27). People with any intellectual dignity, social standing or pride rarely stoop to believe the message of the gospel. God resists the proud and gives grace to the humble.

So the next time you sit next to or talk to someone who professes atheism, don't be at all intimidated. Be encouraged. Here is a shallow thinker who loves his or her sins. You simply have to learn how to address that person's conscience. You do that by imitating Jesus and using His moral Law to bring the knowledge of sin. Then you offer the grace of Christ's death that paid the penalty for that sin and His resurrection that promises eternal life with Him. In the next chapter, we will look at testimonies from a few former atheists who, because someone was willing to share the gospel with them, were able to open their minds to the truth of the gospel and invite Christ into their lives.

ATHEISTS NEED
THE GOSPEL TOO!

Late in 2008, an organization of 11 atheist and "freethinker" groups spent $5,000 to put the message "Don't Believe in God? You are not alone" on 11 billboards in Denver and Colorado Springs. Across the country in Washington, D.C., buses carried a similar message: "Why believe in a god? Just be good for goodness' sake." The American Humanist Association unveiled the $40,000 advertising campaign as a part of their endeavor to bring in more converts to their beliefs. Earlier in the year, the British Humanist Association launched a similar campaign on London buses with the message: "There's probably no God. Now stop worrying and enjoy your life."

It is because of the recent tide of atheism that I asked a couple of my once atheistic friends to share their testimonies. Here is the first:

Having not been raised to believe in God, I didn't. I avoided the subject until my 20s, when curious friends and relatives openly inquired just what it was I believed in, since I didn't go to church or show any signs of faith at all. They assumed I must be an atheist, and I assumed so also. Soon I began justifying my lack of belief by using loci (I thought) to claim God was impossible, too abstract to exist. I started joining any atheist groups I could find and debating Christian acquaintances, especially on the issue of evolution.

Eventually, being an atheist meant having to be well versed in the arguments of the other side; I had to know exactly what it was I claimed to not believe. I read a lot of apologetics books on Christianity and intelligent design. And they made sense! How did the universe and life come into existence and the immensely complex, creative, self-aware human brain? Or even a bacterium or hydrogen atom? The only explanation for it was God.

The second testimony is a bit more comprehensive. Alan Pearson was once a staunch believer that there was no God. Here is his story:

My name is Alan Pearson, and I had all those questions and more. To say I was once a skeptic would be an enormous understatement. I was a super-skeptic. That is, until I met God on a cold predawn February morning in 1992, at age 35, when He answered for me the one burning question I had been asking most of my adult life.

I believe our testimonies should be more about what God has done for us than what the devil did in us, but before I go there, let me tell you about my super-skeptic years.

I never had any real Christian influences in my life. I was not raised in a Christian home. Although my parents were married in a Catholic church, they did not practice, nor did they preach, any religion.

When I was 15 years old, my grandfather died a slow and agonizing death from pancreatic cancer. I was very close to him; he was a great influence on my life. He was a very positive, jovial and robust man, and everyone loved him. After he died, I couldn't figure out if I was mad at God or I was an atheist, because in my mind no truly loving God could allow such a thing to happen to a man like him.

Ultimately I decided I was an atheist, and I stayed there for many, many years. I embraced evolution and other so-called "science" as fact. I lived my life as though there would be no life after death and there were no lasting consequences for my actions. As an atheist, I thought Christians were hypocrites, phony, weak and feeble. It was common for me to make fun of them and their religion. I would say things like, "I'm an atheist, I swear to God." "I avoid church religiously." "I'm giving up church for Lent."

Although I may have been a funny atheist, I wasn't a very good one. Eventually, years later, I became a backsliding atheist, and as a young adult, I mellowed and moved from atheist to skeptic. And I was a super-skeptic! I had all the usual questions:

- What about all the other religions? Could they all be wrong?
- What about the stories in the Bible? Could they all be real?
- What about the different denominations? Didn't they all have their own interpretations of the Bible?

- Which Bible translation was the right one? And why are there so many?
- What about evolution? It seemed plausible and logical to me.
- Where's the proof, the hard evidence, that the Bible is accurate?

More than just questions, my firsthand experiences with the few people I knew who went to church only led me to be even more skeptical and cynical. As I looked at them, their lives and their behavior, I thought, *These people are hypocrites, and I'm as good as they are . . . in fact, I'm better than some of them.* I've heard it said God made man, and then man returned the favor. That's certainly what I did . . . I broke the first Commandment when I made a god in my own image. I thought, *God is surely grading on a curve, and if so, I'm doing pretty well. I mean, compared to Hitler, I'm a saint. A loving God certainly would not condemn me to hell.* I made a god to suit myself.

I was always on the periphery of Christianity . . . without someone to fully explain it, I was left to pick up bits and pieces here and there. Here's one thing I did know about Christianity: whenever I watched a World Series game or the Super Bowl or any other big-time sporting event, there was always some guy behind home plate or on the 50-yard line with a John 3:16 sign. So I thought, *Hey, if that's what it's all about, sign me up, 'cause I want to sit there next year!*

I had seen enough World Series games to be curious about John 3:16, so I found a Bible and I looked it up. It said God "gave" His only Son so I could have eternal life. And that's when I had my biggest question about God. I could not grasp the whole issue of the "sacrifice." I mean, if He's God, what's the big deal? He's God, He can have anything He wants, can't He?

I could not understand how a God, who has everything, who can have everything, could ever make a sacrifice. I thought, *Okay, You gave your Son, but if You truly are God, You can just make another Son. What's the big deal?* And that one question—the question of the sacrifice—haunted me right up until the hour before the hour I first believed.

In January of 1992, my wife, Kim, walked into a church a few blocks from our home to ask for information about the church. We'd both seen this church many times but never discussed it, or any other church—"religion" was just not a part of our lives. She met the pastor that day, and after a brief talk, he sent her home with some reading material. That evening, she shared her story of being "led" to go into the church and her talk with Pastor Chuck. As she shared the reading materials, I was somewhat amazed at her interest level—and, to say the least, I did not share her interest. I held tightly to my cynical and skeptical views of religion and God.

Kim and I had many talks over the next two weeks about my views on churches and religion, and I tried to talk her out of this "religion thing." I calmly explained to her that they only wanted us to join the church so they can get our money. Nonetheless, over that same period, Kim went to several services without me and continued to meet regularly with Pastor Chuck.

One day in early February, Kim came home and declared she wanted to become a member of this church and wanted me to become a member as well. At this point, I could tell there that was no way of talking her out of it. I wasn't sure why, but it was much more than her just being determined about this. It was much bigger. Looking back now, I understand the work the Holy Spirit was doing in her. Little did I know He was about to do a work in me, too.

I agreed to a meeting with Kim and Pastor Chuck. At the meeting, he explained some of the basics of Christianity and Church doctrine. Along with several other couples that were committing to membership at the same time, we enrolled in the requisite weekly classes to become members. However, I did so under silent protest and only to pacify my wife. I was just going along to get along and assuming her religion "phase" would end soon.

Although we attended classes, since I was simply there to please Kim, I wasn't absorbing much of the teaching. One day, Kim brought home a study Bible with a leather case. I had no idea what a "study" Bible was. I had never seen one. The concept of "studying" the Bible was foreign to me—and the thought of actually writing and making notes in a Bible seemed sacrilegious. Or at least as sacrilegious as something could be to a nonbeliever.

My concept of a Bible was built around the huge Bible my mother bought from a door-to-door salesman when I was a kid. That Bible had gold-edged pages and sat on the coffee table. It's a wonder the coffee table did not collapse under the weight of that Bible. I never saw anyone open it.

A few days later, Kim came home with a nifty leather carrying case for my new study Bible. She explained it had a place for my pens, highlighter, notes and so forth. I truly thought she had gone mad.

Because one of the people enrolled in the weekly membership classes worked second shift and could not attend, Pastor Chuck made recordings of each class. In late February, a business trip kept me from attending a class. Ever vigilant, Kim got the tape for me so I could keep up and be prepared for the next class.

At the time, I had a 30-minute commute to work. Interested in me, and not at all interested in God, I thought listening to the tape to and from work would simply be an efficient use of my time. So I plugged in the tape on my way to work on a very cold predawn February morning. This was the morning I would get the answer to my burning question. God knew right where to convict me—right at the heart of the issue I had always questioned: His sacrifice.

As I drove to work very early that morning, I listened to Pastor Chuck describe Christ's last hours. About 15 minutes into the lesson, he went into great detail about the clinical aspects of death by crucifixion—the unbelievable torture and pain, the agonizing slow death. At this point, he wasn't even talking about Christ's crucifixion; he was just talking about death by crucifixion in general. His description was incredibly graphic. The only thing I can compare it to would be *The Passion* movie. However, his description was graphic—so much so that it made the movie tame in comparison. I get sick to my stomach even today, all these years later, just thinking about it.

I will never forget the very moment the Holy Spirit completely washed over me as I drove to work that morning. In an instant, I finally understood God's sacrifice and what it meant to me. I was completely overwhelmed with a flood of emotions simultaneously—I considered pulling off the road because I could barely keep control of the car. On the other hand, I wanted nothing to interrupt this moment. I was completely overcome with grief, guilt, sadness, shame, regret, and yet, at the same time, I was also filled with a sense of joy, forgiveness and hope.

I cannot fully explain it—no one can fully explain supernatural events. All I know is that in that instant my sinful nature was revealed to me. And at the same time, I also knew God's sacrifice, the death of His Son, was the only way I could be reconciled to Him.

Prior to that moment, I never knew how much I had offended God. God has given all of us a conscience, so I knew I had sinned, although I would not have called it that. I knew I had sinned against man, but I had no idea how much my sin had offended God. Prior to that moment, I had no fear of God. I did not know I needed to fear Him and His righteous judgment.

I was like the little girl who sees a flock of sheep in the meadow and says look at how white the sheep look. And against the backdrop of the green grass, they look white. But then it begins to snow, and now the sheep look dirty; they don't look so white after all. That was my story. As I compared myself to others, I looked pretty good. But compared to the pure white snow—compared to the pure white holiness of God—I was filthy and I needed a Savior.

Now I see my sin as God sees it. And now I know there is a judgment to come. And God, in His perfect holiness, will judge all sinners. But for those of us who believe in Jesus and truly repent (that is, turn from our sin), Jesus has already paid for our sin. And now I know I am saved, because I hate the things I used to love and I love the things I used to hate. Even before I had ever heard the term, I knew I had become a "new creation."

As much as I love to tell people my testimony, it seems so inadequate, because mere words can never truly explain what I experienced—the words do not exist. God met me directly where I needed Him, and I have never looked back. He has been the focus of my life ever since and always will be. I am so grateful He convicted my wife and gave her the courage to persist with me as He used her to lead me to Him.

I urge you to share the message of Christ crucified with others. We are commanded to share our faith. If we do not, we are like a fireman who sits outside a burning house and does nothing to rescue the people in the house.

We are all part of the ultimate statistic: 10 out of 10 of us die! Every day 150,000 people die. How many of them slip from life to eternal torment in hell . . . today?

It's no wonder that nonbelievers do not fear hell. Some people would like you to believe that hell is simply a place of separation from God. If they don't want God in this life, what's to fear from not having God in the next life? No, the Bible tells us hell is a place of eternal torment. And we must do all we can to save people from that judgment.

To conclude, let me share a short testimony about an atheist I met recently. I was in New Zealand in March of 2008 at a university where local Christians had organized a debate between an atheist and me. Approximately 150 people showed up, and just before it started, a tall outspoken man named Ryan enthusiastically approached me and said, "I'm honored to meet you. I have watched your videos on the Internet and read your material, and I am really excited about this debate." As he was walking back to his seat, I called out, "Which side are you on?" He replied, "I'm against everything you stand for."

During the question and answer time, Ryan asked some good questions, and I gave my best answers. The next day, he showed up at another meeting at which I was speaking, and he again listened to me for another hour or so at a church service. After the service, we chatted and I signed a copy of *You Can Lead an Atheist to Evidence but You Can't Make Him Think*. We had our photo taken, and Ryan even helped out on our book table. I really cared about Ryan, and was pleased to hear him say at the end of the evening, "Man, why are you so likeable?" The fact that he could feel my love and concern for him was more powerful than any argument I could give him for the existence of God.

Some atheists read everything I write as if I hate them, but even my warning about a place called "hell" springs from love. They accuse me of making money from the sale of my books and the gospel, but I have preached in open-air auditoriums more than 5,000 times and have never been paid. I do that because I love people and care where they spend eternity. If I didn't care, I wouldn't bother with preaching or writing Christian books. I had a successful business before I became a Christian and could have made a good living, but I chose to spend my life pleading with people to consider where they will spend eternity. Doing that has been a small sacrifice, but it is a tangible expression of my love for this dying world. Yet if people refuse to believe that about me, I can't do anything about it.

Most of this world knows that Jesus gave His life on the cross as a sacrifice, but they don't understand *why*. It was a legal transaction. We have violated God's Law through lying, stealing, blasphemy, lust, adultery, hatred, fornication, selfishness and so forth. That Law shows that we are guilty criminals that must stand before the Judge of the Universe. We are heading for God's prison—a terrible place called hell. Yet the gospel tells us that Jesus paid our fine through His sacrifice on the cross. That means that because of the suffering death and resurrection of Jesus of Nazareth, God can legally dismiss our case. He can commute our death sentence and allow us to live upon our repentance and faith in Jesus, because our "fine" was paid 2,000 years ago. This is how the Bible puts it: "But God shows and clearly proves His [own] love for us by the fact that while we were still sinners, Christ (the Messiah, the Anointed One) died for us" (Rom. 5:8, *AMP*).

There's the evidence of His love.

WITNESSING
TO FAMILY

The moment I came to Christ, I was intensely concerned for the salvation of my immediate family. I had found everlasting life, and the members of my family were sitting in the shadow of death. If they died in their sins, they wouldn't just miss out on everlasting life and heaven but also be damned in hell. I could hardly entertain the thought. Nothing consumed me more than that.

I had been using the principles laid out in a four laws booklet to bring my friends to a decision in Christ. I figured that it would simply be a matter of doing the same with my loved ones. But it wouldn't be as easy as I thought. In my ignorance of the nature of sin and of salvation, I led my mom in a sinner's prayer. Of course, there was no knowledge of sin or repentance, and there was no fruit. But worse than that, in my zeal without knowledge, I did more damage than good. I was deeply disappointed when my mom didn't show any signs of regeneration.

Over the following years, I didn't prove to be the normal contemporary Christian. I purchased a huge bus and had massive Scripture verses professionally written on it—about the everlasting life that sinners could find in Christ. I had verses painted onto both sides of my car. I had Scripture painted onto the entire front window of my store. I printed tracts and edited a Christian newspaper called *Living Waters*. I even had a hand-fed printing press in a back room at our house. And I preached the gospel, soapbox style, daily in the heart our city for many years.

My mom was a typical Jewish mom. She loved her little boys. She wouldn't hesitate to ask God if I, and my brother, Phillip, could sit at His right and left hand.

I remember once being closely surrounded by a crowd of about 60 people as someone contended with me about the gospel. I pleaded with him to listen and then held out some literature. If I remember rightly, there were few takers, but I do remember suddenly seeing my mom in the crowd. She stuck out her Jewish-mom hand and took a tract, just because she didn't want to see me humiliated. But she need not have done that. I was used to being abused, ignored, spat at, hated and humiliated. I knew that it wasn't me the crowd hated, but Christ in me.

My dad was always congenial to the gospel. He would follow me around when I preached and agree with everything I said. But he had a character flaw: He started projects but often failed to finish them. He was a carpenter, and yet there were things that were never finished around the house. He was good-natured, and so we joked about this as a family. Unfortunately, this character flaw translated into his walk with God. He believed, but he didn't obey. There was no fruit in his professed Christian walk.

One day, he had a serious heart attack and was rushed to the hospital in an ambulance. After my sister called me from New Zealand during the night, I put down the phone and prayed for him. I felt so weighed down with a sense of empathy for my dear dad that I began to weep. Then I became utterly overwhelmed with emotion. I cried out so loud that Sue came downstairs to see if I was okay.

For two weeks my dad lay in a hospital, and during that time he got things right with God before he died. He finished something that really mattered, and I was unspeakably grateful to God that I would see my beloved dad again.

Pray with Unswerving Faith

I have two siblings. My brother lives in Australia. He jokes about almost everything. When I tried to witness to him, he joked it off. That really upset me. Yet he was never anti-Christian. In fact, he was just the opposite. He would email me when he met a Christian. He would tell them about me and the ministry. He even regularly gave out our million-dollar tract. I would ask myself, *Doesn't he know what's on the back?* I guess he liked the fact that the tract made people laugh.

My sister, Christine, lives in New Zealand. She isn't anti-Christian either. She is a kind, loving sibling who was always around to take care of Mom. Never once did she make me feel guilty for living in another country and not being there to take care of my mom or my dad. However, she sometimes blasphemed like a trooper on steroids.

So there you have it. That's my beloved family, whose salvation I have prayed for every day since I was saved. But I didn't pray that God would simply bless them. I prayed for their eternal salvation, and I have given the issue deep thought to make sure my prayers were heard.

I prayed with faith. Abraham was not staggered at the promise of God through unbelief but was strong in faith and gave glory to God, being fully persuaded that what God had promised He was able to perform. I looked at Jesus' promise in Matthew 21:22, "And whatever things you ask in prayer, believing, you will receive," and I trusted that God was not willing that any perish but that all should come to repentance. I say this reverently, but I believe that God has a soft spot. It's His faithfulness. He is faithful to what He has promised. So, for years I have prayed, "Lord, I rest in Your faithfulness. I thank You for the salvation of my loved ones. I will not stagger at Your promises through unbelief. You are not willing that any perish but that all come to repentance. I rejoice in their salvation. Nothing is impossible for You. All things whatsoever I ask in prayer believing, I shall receive."

I am fully aware that this sort of prayer flies in the face of the theology of some, but I'm not too concerned about that. I know that prosperity preachers have continually used this sort of positive believing prayer for personal wealth. I'm not too concerned about that either. All I am concerned about is the salvation of my loved ones, so I have been praying that way for years. And God honored it with the deathbed salvation of my dad.

Over the years, I have taken Mom to different churches and to special meetings in the hope that the preacher would preach a clear gospel message. It didn't happen. I gave up because not only didn't she hear the gospel but also usually someone with bad breath, teeth missing and a mass of tattoos would hug her and say, "Jesus loves you." That sort of thing freaked her out big-time.

Then something wonderful happened: Ben and Melissa Day became our New Zealand agents. One day, Melissa went around to Mom's house to borrow a banner I had given her. They began talking and became the best of friends. I was so encouraged each time Melissa told me that they had talked about the things of God. I couldn't think of anyone better to talk to her than Melissa, because she was loving and doctrinally sound in the Word. She knew better than to get a "decision" from mom. She loved Mom like her own mother and wanted to see her soundly saved, and she knew that only God could do that.

Oh, Dear

In October of 2008, my sister called me in the United States. She told me that Mom had been taken to the hospital in an ambulance. She was in her mid 80s, and her health was failing. I called the hospital, spoke to her and was delighted that she was coherent. In fact, she was having a great time. She said that she was surrounded by handsome doctors, had good food and was meeting people. She even suggested that she be transferred to the men's ward.

On the day that I called, she tried to tell me how God had taken care of a certain situation. My nephew had found himself in London without a job for three months. Then one day, he walked into a store whose manager was a New Zealander. When my nephew asked about employment, the manager gave him a job immediately. Mom said, "I knew that things would work out. It always does. We get looked after by the Old Boy upstairs." I was horrified. My mom had just called the Almighty God "the Old Boy upstairs."

The next day, my sister called and said that Mom was getting five shots per day. Her blood pressure was through the roof. She couldn't walk or even read. They were seriously concerned about her having a stroke, and they had transferred her to a room that she was sharing with a 96-year-old lady. So there I was. My mom couldn't read. They had put her in a room with a 96-year-old. Melissa had just had a baby, so she was going to be too busy to talk to my mother. Mom couldn't even see well enough to read a Bible. She thought that God was something like a celestial Santa Claus. I had a blaspheming sister and a joking brother. There were very few Christians in New Zealand, let alone ones who shared the gospel and shared it biblically. So I prayed, "Father, I rest in Your faithfulness. With You, nothing is impossible. I thank You for the salvation of my mom, my brother and my sister."

The next day, I called New Zealand and spoke to Mom. She said, "Good things are happening." When I asked what sort of "good things," she said, "There's a 96-year-old lady in my room, and we've been talking about you know what." I said that I did not know what. She said, "About Jesus and God . . . for about three hours. It's *very* interesting."

I started to weep. God is so incredibly faithful! Earlier that day, I had heard a pastor say that he had become saved 36 years ago. Then his dad got saved. Then his mom and his brother and sister came to Christ. I remember thinking how only my dad had come to Christ, and I was feeling a little envious of the pastor.

Mom asked if I wanted to talk to "Nel." I did. Nelly was coherent and said that I once stayed in her house many years ago. I asked, "What are you doing in hospital, Nel?" She said, "I couldn't breathe. It was terrible. I'm all right now, though." Think of it: this dear woman said she couldn't breathe, and yet in the next breath she was talking about the goodness of God and testifying to my unsaved mother. I found out later that she not only prayed for my mom but also laid hands on her as she did so.

Mom was then moved to another hospital where she literally bumped walkers with "Rex," an 84-year-old gentleman. They hit it off from the first collision and became good friends. Then it turned into a budding romance. He had lost his wife five years earlier and was extremely lonely, and he loved Mom's company and her sense of humor.

I called Mom when she was at his house once and asked if he was treating her with respect. She burst into tears and said, "You would not believe how respectfully he treats me!" Then she said, "He's just like you!" She told me that he played hymns on an organ and they prayed together all the time.

So, when you ask God to save your loved ones, trust Him with all of your heart. He is faithful. Show your faith in God by having the peace of mind that He is in total control and that you will see a fulfillment of His promise.

TRUE CONVERSION

As I mentioned in the last chapter, sometimes when we witness to people—even leading them in the sinner's prayer—they do not subsequently exhibit any knowledge of their sin or show signs of true repentance. This can be discouraging. We expect to see immediate changes as a result of a regenerated heart, but we don't see anything different in the way they conduct their lives.

Sadly, not too many people within the contemporary Body of Christ are familiar with what I call "false conversions." Rarely is it taught from modern pulpits that there is such a thing, and yet the Bible is filled with examples of spurious conversions. When Jesus gave the parable of the sower, He likened people's receptivity to the gospel to different kinds of soil. He spoke of a wayside hearer, a stony-ground hearer, a thorny-ground hearer and the genuine convert—the good-soil hearer.

Our churches are filled with false converts. There are people who say they belong to Jesus Christ, but their lives don't match their claims. Listen to what Charles Spurgeon said of this multitude of tares that sit among the wheat:

Who was it that added Judas, and Ananias and Sapphira, and Simon Magus, and Demas to the church? Who was it that stole forth by night and spread tares among the wheat? That evil spirit is not dead, he is still busy enough in this department, and continually adds to the church each as are not saved. His are the mixed multitude which infest the camp of Israel, and are the first to fall a lusting; his the Achans who bring a curse upon the tribes; his are those of whom Jude says, "certain men crept in unawares who were before of old ordained to this condemnation." These adulterate the church, and by so doing, they weaken and defile it, and bring it much grief and dishonor.[1]

Back in August of 1982, by the grace of God, I discovered a biblical truth that God has kindly used to awaken many false converts. I can't think of any greater horror than to think that I'm a Christian and yet on Judgment Day find that I am not. To make it to the gates of heaven and then be thrust into hell is a terror beyond words. Yet that is going to be the fate of multitudes of professing Christians. Listen to the warning Jesus gave about that terrible day:

Many will say to Me in that day, "Lord, Lord, have we not prophesied in Your name, cast out demons in Your name, and done many wonders in Your name?" And then I will declare to them, "I never knew you; depart from Me, you who practice lawlessness!" (Matt. 7:22-23).

These are people who call Jesus "Lord" and yet violate the Ten Commandments. They say they are Christians, but they lie, steal, covet, murder, blaspheme, fornicate, commit adultery and more. I'm sure that if I questioned those people they would say that they don't do such things. But what they fail to realize is that God's Law is spiritual and that if we hate someone, in God's eyes, we have committed murder (see 1 John 3:15). If we lust, we have committed adultery (see Matt. 5:27-28). Our lies may be "white" to us, but to God they will put us in the lake of fire (see Rev. 21:8). Our theft may seem petty, but it can keep us from entering the kingdom of God (see 1 Cor. 6:9-10). None of these sins are slight in the eyes of a holy God.

The Reality of False Conversions

Of all the things we should be sure of in this life, the most important is our eternal salvation. We don't want to be in that mass of deceived people who will cry out, "Lord, Lord." So, for the sake of our own salvation and for the salvation of those to whom we witness, we should be aware of the reality of true and false conversions. The following emails are from people whom God has awakened from such a spurious conversion:

> In a nutshell, I was a false convert for nine years and became a true Christian in October 2007. The problem was that I was 14 years old, and when I prayed the prayer to receive salvation, I didn't understand the depth of my sins. I held on to my faith and belief in Christ but lacked true repentance and a full desire to obey and serve God according to His Word. I did desire greatly to see others saved, because I did believe in hell.
>
> In September 2007, I read *The Way of the Master*. It took me about a month or so to digest what I read from Ray's book, but one day, it finally clicked that what I was reading was not only true, biblical and effective but also that

I probably wasn't a true Christian myself. I don't remember the day or even what I said, but I do know I truly repented of my sins one day in October 2007 and my eyes were opened to the truth.

Contrary to the prosperity gospel message I used to listen to in my false convert days, it's been a rather difficult year of trials since I've become a true Christian. I can't imagine going through this past year without a true faith in Christ. Our recent trial was that my husband and I had to bury our beautiful twin girls. They were born on September 20, 2008. Without the true faith we now have, I imagine we'd be furious with God. Now we aren't angry at God but rejoice in Him that we know our girls are rejoicing with Him now and that someday we will rejoice with them as well!

It hurts beyond what words can express to bury your children, but at least we have our hope in Christ and trust His will! My husband and I cling closer to the cross now and will continue to do so until we finish our race! Our girls have already opened up several opportunities to share the gospel, so praise be to God if that is what their purpose in life was for the brief time we held them here on earth!

Here is another testimony:

I have to tell you about something amazing that just happened to me. I thought it could never happen to me, but it did: *I was born again.* All of a sudden I was given a new heart. I hated sin. I loved God and I believed in Him, not because I knew *about* Him but because I now *knew* Him personally. I established my first real relationship with our heavenly Father and His mediator, Jesus Christ.

Suddenly, all my urges to sin were washed away, and all that I had repented of I turned away from. Lust and lying were *very* frequent sins of mine, and I committed them every day. Many times, I couldn't stop. But with my new heart, I was able to turn away from them, and I haven't done any of those sins for days (something I thought impossible). It is amazing. I've turned away from sin and I have a new heart, ready to serve and glorify the Lord.

All the things that so easily shook my faith do not even dent it now. I know God personally, and I easily believe in every word of the Bible and the promise of His Lord and Savior, Jesus Christ. I am *on fire* for Him now. Thank You, God! I have been reborn! I was a false convert.

Here is one final testimony:

I got saved in February 2007 after hearing "Hell's Best Kept Secret" and "True and False Conversion."[2] I had been a false convert for 21 years of my life, and when I heard these messages, it was as though the stagnant, dark clouds that hovered above me for so long lifted. The reason Jesus had to shed His precious blood, suffer and die made sense to me for the first time.

The seriousness of my sins had not seen the light of day but instead lay cloaked inside my dusty Bible and what I thought were hidden secrets. I had not truly understood anything about God's holiness and His utterly thundering and just hatred of sin. The Law had not been opened and thrust upon me. I took for granted the gift that had been offered through the atoning blood of our precious, mighty, beautiful and wonderful Savior. I had not biblically repented and shed the tears of regret and shame over my callous and cavalier heart.

Yes, I went to church all of my life (inconsistently). Yes, I heard the stories. Yes, I even listened to preaching day after day at my work for the last 3 or 4 years. Yes, I thought I loved Jesus. And yes, I thought I was saved all those years. But something wasn't right, and it frustrated me to no end.

Years of "I can't put my finger on it; what's wrong with me?" vanished when I repented and trusted. I was given a new heart, and it was more obvious to me than an elephant in a parade of fleas. I also understood why all my prayers throughout the years were never answered. They weren't answered because the Lord wasn't even listening to the prayers of the unregenerate, sin-cycling, wicked soul I was (see Prov. 15:29). I even remember saying many times over the years, "I don't think God hears my prayers at all." I realized that for too long I had been a tare among the wheat, a true stony-ground hearer.

It actually scared the wind out of me and made me cry and laugh all at the same time when I understood how blessed I was that God hadn't already ground me into powder. What patience the Lord had with me. I know now that I *will* be in heaven one day, and I know that the Lord saved me and was so kind and gracious to do so. I only want to serve Him and be used by Him for the rest of my days. I don't want to be a "comfortable Christian" but rather an uncomfortable, front-line, battle-worn, in-the-trenches, faithful, faith-filled, headed-for-the-burning-and-crumbling-building servant with skinned knees and a hoarse voice that's been lifted up like a trumpet.

A Common Thread

Do you see a common thread running through these testimonies? After a genuine conversion there is a deep love of God, a love of righteousness, an understanding of sin and of the cross, gratitude and more. These are fruit of salvation. They are not mustered. They grow naturally when a person has been regenerated by the Holy Spirit. This is how Spurgeon says we should examine ourselves to see if we are truly saved:

> Read the Ten Commandments, pause at each one, and confess that you have broken it in either thought or word or deed. Remember that by a glance, we may commit adultery; by a thought, we may be guilty of murder; by a desire, we may steal. Sin is any want of conformity to perfect holiness, and that want of conformity is justly chargeable upon every one of us. Yet the Lord does not, under the gospel dispensation, deal with us according to Law. He does not now sit on the throne of judgment, but He looks down upon us from the throne of grace. . . . Instead of destroying offending man from off the face of the earth, the Lord comes near to us in loving condescension, and pleads with us by His Spirit, saying, "You have sinned, but my Son has died. In Him, I am prepared to deal with you in a way of pure mercy and unmingled grace."[3]

So, how do we know if the person whom we have just led to Christ has experienced a true conversion? How do we know if we have experienced a true conversion in our own lives? Here is a checklist to ensure that we and the person to whom we are witnessing will be in that number when the saints go marching in.

1. *Do I have a knowledge of sin?* I don't mean whether you know that sin *exists* or that you have "sinned" and fallen short of the glory of God in a general sense. I mean, do you see sin in its *true* light—as God sees it. As a Christian, does the thought of not keeping your word (lying) horrify you? Do you grieve when you are tempted to lust (commit adultery in your heart), or covet? Does taking a paperclip or someone else's pen make you tremble because you know that the value of that which you steal is irrelevant? Do you see that *every* time you give in to lust you have committed adultery as far as God is concerned? Does lust distress you as much as it would if you had physically committed adultery? Do you understand that if you hate anyone, you have as good as plunged a knife into his or her back? Do you truly believe that your own heart is deceitful and desperately wicked (see Jer. 17:9)?

2. *Do I have a healthy relationship with God?* Or is it like a marriage that has lost its sparkle? Is that because you have failed to be honest and open in the relationship? No marriage can blossom if there is a lack of faith and open communication. Do you confess your sins to God and ask for His forgiveness the moment you fall rather than

dive into what may be considered a minor sin (an unloving attitude, greed, anger without cause)? Honesty is what keeps joy in our connection to each other in marriage. Nothing will cause you to drift from God like secret sin. But the truth is that there's really no such thing as "secret" sin. God sees every transgression of His Law until it goes under the blood of Christ. So keep the account short. Never let anything build up a wall between you and God and kill your intimacy with Him.

3. *Do I have a concern for the unsaved?* If you don't, you need to be concerned for your own salvation. How can any of us walk by on the other side and let sinners go to hell? How can we say that the love of God dwells in us if we don't care? Do what the Bible says to do—examine yourself. Are you sure you are saved? Is there fruit? If the Holy Spirit dwells in you, there must be a love, a goodness, a kindness that will translate into a concern that will cause you to forget your fears and speak to the unsaved.

4. *Do I have a hunger for God's Word?* Do you rejoice over the promises of God as a person who has found great treasure? Do you read the Bible daily? You should be like a newborn baby who lives to feed and feeds to live. If there is no appetite, then something is desperately wrong. But let me qualify this: There may be times when you excitedly open the Word and other times when you do it out of discipline. But whatever you do, whether you feel like it or not, feed yourself spiritually.

5. *Do I have a passion to live for the will of God?* Have you said, "Not my will, but yours, be done?" Have you done what Scripture tells you to do and presented your body as a living sacrifice to God (see Rom. 12:1-2)? This isn't something you should have to grudgingly do. It should be a joy to do in the light of the cross. If it is grievous to you to bow your knee in submission, you may still be unsaved and not regenerated by the Holy Spirit. If you have been truly born again and you've seen the cross and seen your own sin, you will gladly run back to your father and say, "Make me your hired servant."

6. *Do I discipline myself to pray?* Do you pray without ceasing? Do you talk to God as your closest friend? What do you pray about? Are they prayers steeped in selfishness or soaked in a selflessness? Do your prayers glorify God? Are you seeking first His Kingdom or still building your own?

7. *Do I love other Christians?* Do you rejoice when others are praised? "We know that we have passed from death to life, because we love the brethren. He who does not love his brother abides in death" (1 John 3:14).

8. *Is there praise for God on my lips?* Does worship come naturally to you? Has the Holy Spirit opened your understanding so that any idolatry is gone and you see God as He is—holy, perfect, loving, kind, just and good? When you look at creation, do you see the genius of the Creator's hand, and does that fill your heart with praise?

9. *Do I love Jesus?* Is He precious to you? "If anyone does not love the Lord Jesus Christ, let him be accursed" (1 Cor. 16:22).

10. *Do I preach the cross?* Is it ever before you?

In the light of these thoughts, perhaps each of us needs to go and spend some time alone with God. In fact, I would strongly recommend it. If you were going to jump 10,000 feet out of a plane, wouldn't you check and double-check the straps? How much more should you make sure that you have "put on" the Lord Jesus Christ? This is your eternal salvation we are talking about, so obey the admonition to make your calling and election sure. There's nothing more important than where you will spend eternity.

THE FRUIT OF BIBLICAL EVANGELISM

There is a big difference between modern evangelism and biblical evangelism. The modern gospel makes man, not God, the center object of its message. Man is the one who has something missing in his life. God longs for and even needs his love. The gospel is seen as man's ultimate problem solver. If your marriage is bad, come to Jesus. Is there something missing in your life? Come to Christ. Not happy? Try Jesus. God has a wonderful plan for you, and you will never be happy until you make a decision for Christ.

However, a little study of Scripture and of real life will show you that man can be quite happy without Jesus, enjoying the pleasures of sin for a season. As we have seen, it is this man-centered message that paints him as a victim and God as his celestial Santa Claus that has resulted in our churches being filled with false converts. In truth, man is a criminal and God is his judge. Man is not an unfortunate victim of his circumstances. His heart is wicked and he is in rebellion to the God who gave him life. Jesus didn't come to give man happiness and fill his God-shaped vacuum; He came to give him *righteousness* and save him from being justly damned in hell.

Tragically, the modern Church is not only off in its message but also off in its methods. Biblical evangelism shows that man is so wicked that nothing in him desires God. He hates God without cause (see John 15:25). The Scriptures tell us that no one seeks after God (see Rom. 3:11). But the modern message says that something in man yearns for God. It is God that he is really seeking in his misguided search for happiness.

Biblical evangelism says the only way a wicked sinner can come to God is if God draws him to Himself (see John 6:44). The moral Law has been violated, and before we can even begin to think of a "wonderful plan," its uncompromising demands must be satisfied. God is greatly offended, and the sinner must repent and find peace with God through the blood of the cross. To do this, there must be sorrow for sin—a godly sorrow that results in repentance (see 2 Cor. 7:10). There must also be an understanding of the terrible nature of sin. George Whitefield said, "Before you can speak peace to your hearts, you must be made to see, made to feel, made to weep over, made to bewail, your actual transgressions against the Law of God."

Modern evangelism simply says, "You are a sinner. All have sinned. Jesus died on the cross for you so that you could have real peace. Just give your heart to Him." There is no mention of the Law, Judgment Day, future punishment and the necessity of repentance. The Bible teaches that repentance is God-given. Although man is commanded to repent, he can't do it without the help of God. God *gives* him repentance to the acknowledging of the truth (see 2 Tim. 2:25).

There are many sad byproducts of the modern method, from the drawn-out musical altar-calls that manipulate emotions to the laborers tied up with "follow-up" as they become necessary lifelines between the professed new convert and God.

Tares Among the Wheat

But there is another subtle and tragic result of modern evangelism. Its adherents will say things like, "I led 169 people to the Lord last week. I am so grateful to God for what He's doing." Meanwhile, there you are, faithfully laboring away, using what you believe are biblical methods, but you haven't seen a soul come to Christ. While the adherent of the modern method of evangelism has an abundance of fruit for his labor, you have nothing to show but blood, sweat and tears.

More than likely, the main reason that you don't see "decisions" for Christ is that you fear God, and because of that healthy fear of the Lord, you don't want to lead a single soul into a false profession of faith. You know how easy it is to get decisions and impress people with numbers, but you also know better. It would be easy to say to those who have heard the gospel, "Do you know for sure that your name is written in heaven? Would you like to have that knowledge? I could lead you in a sinner's prayer right now so that you can know that when you die, you will go to heaven. Would you like to pray?" God forbid that you and I would contribute to the numbers of tares who are sitting among the wheat in the contemporary Church.

I preached the gospel for many years almost daily and hardly saw a soul come to Christ. However, after I left New Zealand and came to the United States, I started to hear of ones surrendering to the Savior who had listened to the gospel so long ago. So here is the way to keep yourself encouraged: see your evangelism as sowing in tears (see Ps. 126:5), and then read the following verses over and over until you are familiar with them and understand them:

- John 4:36-38: "And he who reaps receives wages, and gathers fruit for eternal life, that both he who sows and he who reaps may rejoice together. For in this the saying is true: 'One sows and another reaps.' I sent you to reap that for which you have not labored; others have labored, and you have entered into their labors."

- First Corinthians 15:58: "Therefore, my beloved brethren, be steadfast, immovable, always abounding in the work of the Lord, knowing that your labor is not in vain in the Lord."

Never be discouraged. Keep asking God that you may see fruit for your labors, but don't let seeing fruit now be your source of encouragement and motivation. Let the motivation be that God is faithful to watch over His Word. There's nothing wrong with the seed of the gospel, and it's up to God to bring it to life in each person in His perfect timing.

A Reminder of God's View

Manuel, a Russian-speaking Mexican brother who moved from Canada with his Russian wife to live in France, spoke fluent French and English. Daniel (my son) and Mark Spence (my manager) and I were in Paris for five days, and having Manuel to interpret for us sure was helpful. We filmed under the Eiffel Tower and around other well-known places in the city, including the amazing Notre Dame Cathedral and the Arc de Triomphe. I spoke three times at a large and lively church—there was even an overflow of people sitting in the parking lot.

Believers in the theory of evolution have often encouraged me to visit museums to see proof of transitional forms, so the next day a group of us visited the prestigious evolution museum (Grande Gallerie de l'Evolution) in Paris, which was packed full of stuffed animals that God had created. But we couldn't find anything about evolution. We searched for about an hour, and then finally asked authorities for the evolution section. It turned out to be a stuffed image of the discredited "Lucy" and a copy of Charles Darwin's book *Origin of Species*. It was underwhelming. From there, we went to the amazing Louvre Museum. I have often said that I love going through a museum as long as I am on a motorbike. It's not that I don't like seeing stuff, but I can see everything in the display in two seconds. But the Louvre is breathtaking. It has thousands of incredible paintings that are hundreds of years old. We even had the thrill of doing a witnessing interview in front of the Mona Lisa.

When we arrived back at our hotel, Manuel came to our room for fellowship. Daniel was looking up something on his laptop computer, so I told him to show Manuel our ministry in Southern California. Through the miracle of the Internet, Daniel was able to pull up our security cameras and look throughout the building in real time. We could see our workers in the ministry going about various jobs as it was actually happening. As we were watching, the FedEx truck pulled up and the driver approached the door and rang the bell. He waited and waited. Then we could see from his body language that he was getting upset. I grabbed a cell phone and called the ministry, and when a worker answered,

I said, "It's Ray here. I'm calling from Paris, France. We are looking at the security cameras, and the FedEx driver is at the door. The bell isn't working, so you better run down and let him in." Ten seconds later, we saw the door open and a staff member wave at the camera and explain to the FedEx man what was going on. It was amazing experience for all of us.

God sees every FedEx man at every door. He knows every hair on every head of every person that has been born. He sees every thought of every mind and hears every beat of every human heart. He even sees every atom of every drop of blood that pumps though every artery of every body. He is not bound by time or by space. He sees everything, knows everything and can do anything . . . everything but sin. While this is mind-blowing, it should console us to know that He is with us and no longer against us. But more than that, it should console us that He is our helper when it comes to reaching the lost. We are weak, but He is strong. We don't know a moment into the future, but He does. He sees when we fail. He sees when we are faithful.

Plane Speaking

On the airplane ride home from Paris to Los Angeles, I sat next to a man who was older, bigger and better dressed than I was. Normally I feel intimidated by such individuals when I am sitting next to them on a plane. These are the sorts of people who get the armrest and you don't even battle them for it. I'm sure you have your nemesis. Big, rich, older businessmen are mine. Give me a young atheist who has been to a university and I am ready to spar, but not this type. Of course, usually it's just my imagination that is being fueled by my fears, and Mr. Rich Businessman turns out to be congenial.

But this was not the case for the man I had just sat beside on the plane. He was proving to be my biggest nightmare. My initial warm greeting had been met with dry ice. There wasn't the warmth to even kindle the slightest spark of a conversation. So, for the next eight hours, I wrestled with my fears and my lack of love for him.

Adding to my thoughts was a sense of repulsion toward the horrible-sounding cough he had. It physically turned my stomach. Each cough (and there were hundreds) had the echo of a deep, breath-taking gurgle. I felt shallow in my concern for his salvation. I thought about his children and the possibility they may be Christians who were earnestly praying for their beloved dad, and here I was chickening out when it came to sharing the gospel with him.

I decided I would offer him a tract at the end of the flight, and I began reading a Christian magazine that talked about how evolutionary proponents were replacing "B.C." (before Christ) with "B.C.E." (before common era). Mr. Death Cough was now intensely playing on-screen solitaire. He had been at it for a while and was uttering the same four-lettered cuss word every time he misplayed. I was sickened by his loud and unashamed dirty speech. Each cuss-word made me think about his godlessness and his eternal fate.

Finally, I couldn't stand it any longer. I had to try to witness to him. I earnestly prayed, "Lord, if You want me to witness to this man, please have him stop playing this game." To my horror, he stopped about five seconds after I prayed. I immediately said a chirpy, "Enjoy that, huh? So, what do you do for a living?"

"I'm a contractor."

"Have you been doing that for long?"

"Since Christ was born," he answered.

Since Christ was born? My eyes widened, and I had to smile at his answer. I boldly asked, "What's your name?"

"Sheen."

"Sheen, I have a question for you. Do you think there's an afterlife?"

"Interesting question . . . I don't know."

"Do you think there's a heaven? Or do we get reincarnated?"

"I think I will come back as something."

"Do you know what you will come back as?"

"Nope."

"If there's a heaven, do you think you are good enough to go there?"

"Yes, I am."

When I next asked if I could question him about his goodness, out came the dry ice. He said he didn't want to talk any further, so I mumbled, "I tried," and decided to leave him to his coughing and cussing. I did have a warm consolation. I no longer felt the plaguing of my conscience. I also had the consolation that success isn't about getting a decision for Christ or even sharing the whole gospel. Success is simply doing my best to obey God.

Who knows, maybe 40 people had already witnessed to Sheen and my few words would be the straw that broke the camel's back. How many times we hear testimonies of people coming to Christ and relating how everywhere they went it seemed that someone said something to them about God!

Sheen went back to his game, but he seemed to have lost his intensity, and he also stopped his cussing.

Open-Air Schooling

Each month during summer, a group of die-hard (biblically normal) Christians come from around the world for three days of intensive training through our academy.[1] The first day is simply food, fellowship, fun and lots of practical teaching—from Kirk, myself and our capable and experienced team.[2]

The second day is open-air preaching in Hollywood. This is where the rubber meets the road. It's a case of sink or swim. We have learned about the waters of evangelism, and now it's time to jump in off the deep end. These people come to the academy knowing that.

I am always amazed that more than 90 percent of those who attend our training session actually break the "sound barrier" and preach open air. They have the incredible privilege of going home knowing that they preached the everlasting gospel in the last days and that they did it in famous Hollywood. One nervous man said, "If I can do it in Hollywood, I can do it in good old Ohio." He is right. Most return home and make witnessing and open-air preaching a way of life.

One such outreach session took place on Halloween, October 31, 2008. I wasn't excited about going to Hollywood that day. It's bad enough with all the people in weird costumes posing for pictures for money without adding Halloween to Hollywood. For that reason I hesitated to pick up my camera, though I usually take it with me to each Academy outreach to get witnessing encounters. I picked it up anyway, thinking that I would regret it if I missed a really good interview because I didn't take it.

We arrived in Hollywood, spent about 20 minutes in McDonalds fueling up, and then walked toward where the group was now preaching. Suddenly, my cell phone rang. It was Scotty, my radio technician, and he wanted to link up to show me something. We found each other, and he then nodded toward a man with a slight potbelly who was holding a Bible and listening to the preaching.

Scotty whispered, "That's him. I would know him anywhere. He is the big guy in the gang Kirk witnessed to on the Santa Monica Pier." Five years earlier, Kirk and I and our film crew were interviewing people on the pier when Kirk quickly ran across to what looked like a group of hardened gang members. They had their shirts off, showing their tattoos, and with their shaven heads they sure looked tough. One camera kept rolling as Kirk spoke to them for about 10 minutes, and then we carried on with the other one-to-one interviews.

That night, I checked out the footage. It was amazing. Captivating. These guys were tough as nails. Kirk's innocent demeanor stood out in contrast as he befriended them, took them through the Law into grace and pleaded with them to get right with God. A week or so later, after Duane Barnhardt (our brilliant producer/director) had edited the sequence and put sound onto it, it was even more riveting. It had passion, drama, humor and tension, all in about 10 minutes. It became the most outstanding witnessing sequence on our television program, airing in 70 countries and on 31 networks.[3] Hundreds of thousands viewed it on YouTube.[4]

One of the highlights was when Kirk said, "Jesus said, 'You have heard it said by them of old "You shall not commit adultery." But I say to you, whoever looks at a woman to lust after her has committed adultery already with her in his heart.'" Suddenly, a shirtless gang member with a big pot belly and dark sunglasses stepped forward, and with an angry look on his face, said, "Jesus did not say that!" You could feel the tension. The music added to the drama, as it looked like beloved Mike Seaver was about to get beaten up by a drunken thug. And now Scotty was saying that this was the same man—Potbelly.

I said, "No, it's not. The guy looked different." Scotty said, "I will bet you anything you like that it's him." I was sure that it wasn't, so I approached the man and said, "Excuse me, sir. Were you ever a gang member?" The man looked taken aback and said that he wasn't and that he was a Christian. I looked over at Scotty and said, "It's not him. The man was never a gang member, and he's a Christian."

Scotty didn't flinch. He had a picture of Kirk in his hand and held it up for the man to see. He said, "Did you ever get witnessed to with a group of guys on Santa Monica Pier by this guy?" The man said, "Yes. He spoke to us five years ago on the Santa Monica Pier."

I was flabbergasted.

I grabbed my camera and said, "May I interview you for our television program?" Within minutes, I was hearing the inside story. The man's name was Alvie. The "gang" was actually two of his nephews and their friends. He said that he was drunk at the time, and he sincerely apologized. He also said that he had a potbelly back then and explained why he was a little uptight when I asked him if he was ever in a gang. He thought that I was trying to get him to join one.

Five months earlier, some Christians had picked him up off the streets and taken him to a Bible study at the famed Los Angeles "Dream Center." He now had been soundly saved and was reading his Bible every day. He said that at the time Kirk witnessed to them, the gang leader (named Mario) was into burglary, robbery, drugs and alcohol and was living on the streets. God had saved him, too, and he was now happily married and had children.

Alvie was almost weeping with sincerity as he testified to God's goodness in saving him from sin. It's interesting that you can change the name "Alvie" around a little and you get the word "alive." That's what God had done to this dying sinner: made him alive in Christ.

After the interview was finished, I walked across to Scotty, hugged him and said, "I am so sorry for not believing you. How did you know it was him?" Scotty said that it was the side of Alvie's mouth that did it. He lifted it slightly in the gang footage, and Scotty saw him doing it as he watched the open-air preaching. Scotty is a tech man. He's into those sorts of details.

There are about 11 million people in Southern California, scattered over 100 cities, and God let us meet up with Alvie, the fruit of a labor five years earlier. God knows how and when to encourage us. So *never* be discouraged if you are sowing in tears. One person sows and another reaps, but it's God who gives the increase.

You Have Been Called

Do you like mysteries? I have one for you. Look at the following Scripture closely:

> When He had stopped speaking, He said to Simon, "Launch out into the deep and let down your nets for a catch." But Simon answered and said to Him, "Master, we have toiled all night and caught nothing; nevertheless at Your word I will let down the net." And when they had done this, they caught a great number of fish, and their net was breaking. So they signaled to their partners in the other boat to come and help them. And they came and filled both the boats, so that they began to sink. When Simon Peter saw it, he fell down at Jesus' knees, saying, "Depart from me, for I am a sinful man, O Lord!" (Luke 5:4-8).

Peter fished all night and caught nothing. Why would anyone fish *all night*? Were finances tight? Couldn't he sleep? He had no trouble later sleeping in the Garden of Gethsemane. He toiled all night casting the net, pulling it in, finding nothing and then casting it out again. From there, it is easy to get the idea that it was when he listened to Jesus that he caught fish. And from there we can understand that it's only when we listen to the Master that we will catch men. We have churches across the world that every week cast their modern nets and catch nothing.[5] That's because without reference to the Law, they are fishing in the dark.

The name "Peter" means "small stone." A lot can be done with an insignificant stone that sits among billions of others on this earth. A cold and hard inanimate stone once saved a nation from defeat. It was picked up from among others in a brook and placed in the sling of a young shepherd boy, and its course was guided by the hand of Almighty God (see 1 Sam. 17).

Peter was handpicked from among billions of other small stones. He was an insignificant fisherman with an unregenerate heart of stone, until his brother Andrew found him and told him that he had found the Messiah (see John 1:40). That was when Jesus said, " 'You are Simon the son of Jonah. You shall be called Cephas' (which is translated, a Stone)" (v. 42). It would seem that this was the first thing that Jesus said to Peter, and then 40 days later, He called him to follow Him and fish for men.

In this incident, however, we are told that the reason Andrew brought his brother to Jesus was because he himself had spent the day with Jesus after he had heard John say, "Behold! The Lamb of God!" (John 1:29). So, John the Baptist hadn't yet been put in prison by Herod. When reading the Scriptures, it's easy to get the impression that the first time that Peter saw Jesus was when he was cleaning his nets, and that when he saw Jesus and heard Him say, "Follow me," he dropped everything and followed Him. But that wasn't the case. Peter had time to think about his time with Jesus before he followed Him. In Matthew 4:18-19, we are told:

> And Jesus, walking by the Sea of Galilee, saw two brethren, Simon called Peter, and Andrew his brother, casting a net into the sea; for they were fishermen. Then He said to them, "Follow Me, and I will make you fishers of men."

This incident happened *after* Jesus had been baptized by John and had spent 40 days and 40 nights fasting in the wilderness (see John 4:1-2). So again, Peter had about six weeks to think about his encounter with Jesus before he left everything to follow Him. That's significant. Remember, Peter didn't have what you and I have. He didn't have the knowledge of the New Testament. He hadn't seen any miracles, and he didn't have the knowledge of the cross. Perhaps Peter was ready to follow Jesus from the moment he met Him, but he wasn't *called* to follow Him that day.

The average Christian can identify with Peter. We are called "lively stones." We have been handpicked from among millions for the purposes of God. We have been saved to serve, and it should be our prayer that the Almighty God will guide every move we make through this life.

It took five years for our team to see the fruit with Mario and Alvie. You may not see any from your labors until eternity. But if you will see your "success" as simply sowing, then you will be content to sow, because you know that God is faithful.

So keep laboring. He will do the rest.

ICING ON THE CAKE

In October of 2008, Ray and I were on our way to speak at a Transformed conference when I said that it would be fun to go to a local theater and stand up and preach the gospel to the audience at the end of *Fireproof*. The movie had just been released and was into its second weekend, so that's what we did. With the management's permission, we (and 14 other people from our team) entered the theater in the dark about 30 minutes before the film's end and discreetly sat down in the back.

Just before the end of the film, we walked down to the front, and I stood up and introduced myself. You could have heard a pin drop. It was so much fun. I spoke about some of the highlights of the movie and explained that the woman I kissed in it wasn't my on-screen wife. She was my real wife, who had been specially flown in for the kiss as a stunt double (perhaps the first of its kind for Hollywood). Then I introduced Ray, and he preached the gospel. It was as much a delight for us to speak as it was for the audience to see the movie's hero come to life.

As we made a quick exit, a tall man in his thirties ran after us and said that he wanted to surrender his life to Christ. We gently grilled him as to his motives. Did he see himself as a sinner? Did he understand the cross? Was he truly giving up his love of sin and yielding his will to God? It seemed evident that he was, so we told him to confess his sins, and then we prayed for him.

It was sweet icing on the cake that night. We couldn't help but think about how Jesus said there is great joy in heaven when one sinner repents. We shared in a little of that joy that night.

—Kirk Cameron

POSTSCRIPT

A FEW PRACTICAL TIPS ON SHARING YOUR FAITH

BY EMEAL ("E.Z.") ZWAYNE

Emeal ("E.Z.") Zwayne is the executive vice president of Living Waters Publications. Make sure you listen to his "Passing the Torch" CD (which has been referred to as a life-changing teaching) available through www.livingwaters.com (click on the "store" link and then the "audio" link).

Now that you have finished reading *Conquer Your Fear, Share Your Faith,* you understand that each of us has been commanded to *go* into all the world and share the gospel. But how exactly do we accomplish this? One approach is door-to-door evangelism—but it can be extremely nerve-racking. Just the thought of walking up to a stranger's door to share the gospel is enough to send the bravest of us into a severe panic attack, or at least hyperventilation. However, for those who are so inclined, this is a wonderful opportunity to present the soul-saving gospel of our Savior. If you're willing to be used by the Lord in this way, I've provided a few tips to help you in the process.

Round Up Helpers

When going door-to-door, a great way to get people's attention is to begin by offering to do small handyman chores for free. This gesture is an effective way to demonstrate your care and concern for your neighbors.

To round up the necessary helpers, first put out two sign-up sheets at your church and make an announcement to the congregation. Explain that you are seeking people who are interested in using their handyman skills to freely serve the community when called on during an occasional weekend. Emphasize that their participation will be minimal and rarely required (we have found that while most people sincerely appreciate the gesture to serve them, very few will ever call to request assistance). Also state that you are looking for people who are interested in witnessing door to door.

Once you have a reasonable number of people signed up (5 to 10, depending on your church size), specify a regular time and place that the witnessing team will meet each week (or however often you decide to go out).

Make a Plan

You will then need to map out the homes in your community. It's good to be systematic about your approach and keep records of every address, jotting down the names of people you speak with and the responses you receive. This will come in handy for future visitations. If your church doesn't have brochures or calling cards, don't forget to print up some cards containing the church contact information, address and other necessary information so that people can respond to your offer.

After assembling your teams, mapping out the homes in your community and gathering the necessary materials (including the questionnaire—see below), you are ready to begin. Always be sure to send people out in teams of two—no less (for their safety), and preferably no more (you don't want to intimidate people by appearing in a gang at their door!).

Prepare a Conversation-Starter

When you approach each door, you will need to have an idea of how you will begin the conversation. I recommend that you begin by saying something to this effect:

Hi, how are you today? I'm sorry to bother you at your home. I'll make this really quick. My name is _____ and this is my friend, _____. We're from _____, a local Christian church. We're not here to sell you anything or to get you to come to our church. We just wanted to let you know that we have a ministry set up to freely serve the community.

So, if you are ever doing any handyman work around your home—like painting, major gardening, putting up a fence—we have a team of people from our church who are eager to come out and help you. There is no charge, and absolutely no donations are accepted. And let me assure you that there are no strings attached. We just want to be a blessing to you. Here is a card with our contact information. Please don't ever hesitate to call us. It would be our pleasure to serve you in any way we can.

We're also conducting a quick questionnaire today. It's only three short questions and will take only two to three minutes. Would that be okay?

Conduct a Questionnaire

At this point, most people will be overwhelmed and blessed by your offer to freely serve them and open to participate in the questionnaire. The questionnaire should contain the following questions:

1. Do you believe in the existence of any type of god or higher power?

2. I'm sure you've heard of something called "Judgment Day." This is said to be the day when everyone will be judged by God and receive either heaven or hell for all eternity. If there truly was a coming Day of Judgment, do you think it would be important for people to know what they would need to do in order to go to heaven and avoid hell?

3. Because you believe this to be important [or, if they do not think it is important, say, "If you happen to be wrong and there is indeed a coming Judgment Day . . ."] do you think you would know what a person would need to do in order to go to heaven and avoid hell? If so, what would you say that is?"

You should summarize these questions on a printed questionnaire; however, it's important for members of the witnessing team to memorize these questions if possible rather than read them. They should glance down at the questionnaire only for a second, just to remember the gist of each question, and then look the person in the eye when communicating.

On the questionnaire, place two columns beside each question where the team member can mark a yes or no. It's not necessary to write down the person's answer about how someone can go to heaven and avoid hell. If anyone asks why you're conducting the questionnaire, the honest answer should be: "We are conducting this questionnaire to familiarize ourselves with the overall spiritual perspective of our community."

Ask Follow-up Questions

Once the questions have been asked, most people will begin to open up and share their opinions. It is very important that you listen attentively and closely at this point.

After they have finished sharing, transition by saying something such as, "Thank you so much. That concludes the questionnaire, but I have a couple of quick additional questions to ask you on a personal level. Would you consider yourself to be an open-minded person?" Let the person respond. Then ask, "Do you respect other people's beliefs?"

The overwhelming majority of people will answer yes to these two questions. From that point, you can springboard into the gospel by saying, "I'm glad to hear that. Before we go, let me quickly tell you what we believe about the coming Day of Judgment and what you can do to go to heaven and avoid hell, since this is the most important matter in the world."

During the conversation, you can refer back to the fact that the person said he or she was open-minded and respectful of other people's beliefs in order to reinforce what you are saying. We've found this to be quite effective.

My team and I have used this approach at approximately 1,000 homes and with countless people throughout the years on the street and in public places. By God's grace, it has been a fruitful approach and has enabled us to share the gospel of salvation with many unsaved people

While this is a good and proven format, remember that it is important to be flexible regarding the actual words that are used. This is simply meant to be a helpful guideline, so be sure to use the words with which you are most comfortable.

May the Lord bless you as you go, and may He open doors that no man can shut.

EVANGELISM CRASH COURSE
STUDENT GUIDE

WELCOME!

The following study guide is designed to be used in conjunction with the *Conquer Your Fear, Share Your Faith* Evangelism Crash Course. This four-session course designed by Kirk and I will walk you through the principles in this book, and it features a DVD presentation with our on-the-street encounters as we have been out witnessing to people.

When I first stood up to preach in the open air, I wouldn't say that I was "fearful." I was utterly mortified. But with the help of God, I was able to get up and conquer that fear. Since that day way back in 1975, I have preached open air more than 5,000 times, and I still have to fight fear. But each time I get up and speak, I conquer the fear because I share my faith. It is important to understand that this course will not rid you of fear (it may even introduce you to it), but it will give you weapons that will give you courage so you can effectively fight the good fight of faith.

Kirk and I hope this will be one of the most powerful, eye-opening events of your life. Perhaps you have tried to share your faith and become discouraged or disillusioned by people's responses. Like countless others through the ages, you will find, as we have, that using the biblical principles in this book will revolutionize your life and witness. This is not some new method that we have devised; it is a timeless truth firmly rooted in the pages of Scripture, validated by centuries of Church use and proven by our own practice for more than 20 years.

By following these principles, you will learn how to share your faith simply, effectively and biblically . . . the way Jesus did. All you need is a desire to obey God—and to follow in the footsteps of Jesus.

We pray that today you will get the tools and the courage you need to become an active and effective soul winner in the harvest field. Whether you are already extensively involved in the Great Commission or just desire a deeper commitment, we pray that the Lord will give you a greater love for sinners and an *urgency* for lost souls today.

God bless you,

Ray Comfort

THE LOVE TEST

Take this test before the first video teaching.
With an honest heart, contemplate each statement.

1. The thought of sharing my faith:
   a. Terrifies me
   b. Embarrasses me
   c. Excites me
   d. Bores me

2. I believe that the person with whom I share my faith would probably:
   a. Thank me
   b. Physically attack me
   c. Think I'm a fanatic
   d. It doesn't matter what they do to me

3. A person who is not born again will:
   a. Be eternally happy
   b. Die unfulfilled
   c. Still go to heaven
   d. Spend eternity in hell

4. The fact that anyone could suffer in hell forever:
   a. Doesn't worry me
   b. Concerns me
   c. Horrifies me
   d. Isn't my problem

5. I could conquer my fears about sharing my faith if each time I tried I was given:
   a. $20
   b. $100
   c. $1,000
   d. A promise that God would be with me

6. According to Colossians 1:28, we are told that we should be warning:
   a. All Jews
   b. Our relatives
   c. Every person
   d. Every Christian

7. In light of that command, I have been:
   a. Disobedient
   b. Faithful
   c. Unaware of my responsibility
   d. Complacent

8. I am:
   a. An on-fire Christian who will use any possible way to reach the lost with the gospel
   b. Neither hot nor cold, but lukewarm (see Rev. 3:16)
   c. Not sure if my love for Christ is strong enough (see John 14:15)

9. If I saw a blind man walking toward a 1,000-foot cliff, I would immediately:
   a. Offer him my favorite Christian CD
   b. Invite him to my house for a non-confrontational BBQ the following weekend

   c.   Suggest a more fulfilling place to walk

   d.   Warn him about the cliff

10. When Paul pleaded with the people on Mars Hill (see Acts 17), he demonstrated his concern for them by:

   a.   Inviting them to a worship service in the upper room

   b.   Smiling and hoping they noticed the peace in his eyes

   c.   Saying something to make them feel good about themselves

   d.   Telling them about the coming Day of Judgment and what they must do to be saved

11. If we know someone who is not born again, we should do all we can to:

   a.   Spend months building their trust and hope they ask us what makes us different (assuming they don't die first . . . which we can't assume)

   b.   Invite them to church and hope that they will want to come back

   c.   Wear a cross around our neck so they'll know we're sold out for Jesus

   d.   Learn to go to them in love and compassion, speaking the truth, leading them to the Savior

12. In light of the fact that 150,000 people die every day, and I know how to cure death, what would I like to do now?

   a.   Pray about it

   b.   Leave this training session before it even gets started

   c.   Begin to learn how to share my faith, effectively, biblically—the way Jesus did—and reach the lost with the gospel

SESSION 4

"THE FIREFIGHTER"

An experienced New York firefighter was charged this week with grave neglect of duty. Prosecutors maintained that he abandoned his responsibility and betrayed the people of New York when he failed to release rescue equipment. This resulted in the needless and tragic deaths of a family of five.[*]

NOTES:

_____

_____

_____

_____

_____

_____

_____

_____

_____

_____

_____

_____

_____

_____

_____

_____

_____

_____

Session 4 Quiz

1. How did you react as you heard the firefighter's story? What did the firefighter do that was wrong?

    _____

    _____

    _____

    _____

2. Can you think of any justification for his lack of concern?

    _____

    _____

    _____

    _____

3. Was the fire chief justified in dishonorably discharging the firefighter from the fire department? What sentence did you give the firefighter?

    _____

    _____

    _____

    _____

4. Who are the people in your life whose salvation you are most concerned about?

    _____

    _____

    _____

    _____

5. Why are you concerned?

_____

_____

_____

_____

_____

6. What are you doing about it?

_____

_____

_____

_____

_____

7. With whom do you find it more difficult to share the gospel: family and friends, or complete strangers? Why?

_____

_____

_____

_____

_____

8. How would you describe your current attitude about the fate of the lost: (a) unconcerned; (b) concerned; (c) alarmed; (d) horrified? Why?

_____

_____

_____

_____

_____

9. Did you find it helpful to see someone on the program witnessing? Why or why not?

_____

_____

_____

_____

_____

Conclude by writing a letter to God. Say something like, "God, these are my hopes and desires for this course. This is what I'm afraid of and this is what I'm hoping You'll do in me." Then write out what you want to see God do in your life through these lessons. Seal it in an envelope and place your name on it. No one is going to read it. Give it to the leader for safekeeping. It will be returned to you at the end of the course, and you will then see how God answered your prayers. Be sure to do this because it will be a very meaningful experience when you graduate.

---

*   Although there have been incidents similar to this, this particular incident didn't happen. It is parabolic.

SESSION 2

HELL'S BEST KEPT SECRET

Why do 80 to 90 percent of those making a decision for Christ fall away from the faith? What is the principle that Spurgeon, Wesley, Whitefield and other great preachers used to reach the lost? Why has the Church neglected it? Get ready to discover what Charles Spurgeon called "our ablest auxiliary"—that is, our most powerful weapon!

NOTES:

_____

_____

_____

_____

_____

_____

_____

_____

_____

_____

_____

_____

_____

_____

_____

_____

Session 2 Quiz

1. What is it that the Bible says is "perfect, converting the soul"? (See Ps. 19:7.)

   _____

   _____

   _____

   _____

   _____

2. According to Romans 3:19-20, Romans 7:7 and Galatians 3:24, what are four functions of the Law?

   1. _____
   2. _____
   3. _____
   4. _____

3. What is the biblical definition of sin? (See 1 John 3:4.)

   _____

   _____

   _____

   _____

   _____

4. What does the word "conscience" mean?

   _____

   _____

   _____

   _____

5. What did modern evangelism choose to use to attract sinners to the gospel?

_____

_____

_____

_____

6. What was the first passenger told about the parachute?

_____

_____

_____

_____

7. What was the result of his experience?

_____

_____

_____

_____

8. What was the second passenger told?

_____

_____

_____

_____

9. What was the result of his experience?

_____

_____

_____

_____

10. What should we be telling the "passengers"?

_____

_____

_____

_____

_____

11. Who is the Law designed for (see 1 Tim. 1:9-10)?

_____

_____

_____

_____

_____

BONUS: How many of the Ten Commandments can you name by memory?

1. _____
2. _____
3. _____
4. _____
5. _____
6. _____
7. _____
8. _____
9. _____
10. _____

Session 2 Quiz Answers

1. The Law of the Lord is perfect converting the soul. Matthew Henry says, "Nothing is to be added to it nor taken from it. It is of use to convert the soul, to bring us back to ourselves, to our God, to our duty; for it shows us our sinfulness and misery in our departures from God and the indispensable necessity of our return to him."

2. Four of the functions of God's Law for humanity are: (1) it stops the sinner's mouth from justifying itself; (2) it makes the whole world realize that they are guilty; (3) it brings the knowledge of sin; and (4) it acts as a schoolmaster to bring us to Christ.

3. The biblical definition of sin is transgression of the Law. This is the definition of sin in general. The Greek word "sin" (*hamartia*) is literally "a missing of the mark" (God's perfect Law is the mark that we must aim for). Romans 3:20 tells us, "By the law is the knowledge of sin." The straight edge of a ruler shows the crookedness of a line.

4. The word "conscience" means "with knowledge." Con means "with" and science means "knowledge."

5. Modern evangelism has chosen to attract sinners by using "benefits." Life enhancement is now the drawing card to bring someone to Christ, with something like this: "You will never find true happiness until you come to the Lord. You have a 'God-shaped vacuum' that only He can fill. God will heal your

marriage and take away that addiction problem. He'll get you out of financial trouble and be your best friend."

6. The first passenger was told that the parachute would improve his flight.

7. He put the parachute on for the wrong reason. He became disillusioned and somewhat embittered against the person who gave him the parachute, and quite rightly so. He was promised the parachute would improve the flight and all he got was embarrassment and humiliation.

8. He was told the parachute would save his life.

9. The second passenger didn't notice the extra weight upon his shoulders or the fact that he couldn't sit upright. He was able to withstand the mockery of the other passengers because he didn't put the parachute on for a better flight, but rather to escape the jump to come. Everything else just paled in comparison to the horrific thought of having to jump without the parachute.

10. We should be telling the other passengers they have an appointment with death they will not miss. Unless they repent and put on the Lord Jesus Christ, they will die in their sins. They need to know they are enemies of God through their wicked works and that God will judge them in righteousness.

11. The Law is designed for lawbreakers and rebels, the ungodly and sinful, the unholy and irreligious; for those who kill their

fathers or mothers, for murderers, for adulterers and perverts, for slave traders and liars and perjurers—and for whatever else is contrary to the sound doctrine.

BONUS answer:
1. You shall have no other gods before Me.
2. You shall not make for yourself an idol.
3. You shall not take the name of God in vain.
4. Remember the Sabbath day to keep it holy.
5. Honor your father and your mother.
6. You shall not murder.
7. You shall not commit adultery.
8. You shall not steal.
9. You shall not bear false witness (lie).
10. You shall not covet.

SESSION 3
TRUE & FALSE CONVERSIONS

This message explains why there are so many problems with divorce, alcohol and drug use, abortion, and immorality within Christendom today. Are our churches really filled with true believers? This teaching is foundational, and goes hand-in-hand with session 1. It is important that you understand this material, as it will have a great bearing on how you spend your time and how you share the principles of God's Word. If you have ever wondered why so much of the Church looks and acts just like the world, you'll love this teaching.

NOTES:

_____
_____
_____
_____
_____
_____
_____
_____
_____
_____
_____
_____
_____
_____
_____
_____
_____

Session 3 Quiz

1. What damage can be done by a Christian who doesn't understand that there is such a thing as a false conversion?

   _____

   _____

   _____

2. What did Jesus say to His disciples when they questioned Him about the Parable of the Sower?

   _____

   _____

   _____

3. In the Parable of the Sower, what are the six characteristics of a false convert?

   1. _____

   2. _____

   3. _____

   4. _____

   5. _____

   6. _____

4. What light does James 2:19 shed on the sixth characteristic of a false convert?

   _____

   _____

   _____

   _____

5. What are the five fruits of a true convert?

  1. _____
  2. _____
  3. _____
  4. _____
  5. _____

6. What are the three things that happen here on earth to expose false converts?

_____
_____
_____
_____
_____

7. When will the false convert ultimately be exposed?

_____
_____
_____
_____
_____

8. Name some parables that Jesus told that speak of true and false conversions.

_____
_____
_____
_____
_____

9. How can we, as evangelistic Christians, make sure we are not responsible for bringing false converts into the Church?

_____

_____

_____

_____

_____

BONUS: What "false" person do the following verses warn us about?

Matthew 7:15
Mark 13:22
2 Corinthians 11:13
Galatians 2:4
2 Peter 2:1

Session 3 Quiz Answers

1. The damage done by a Christian who doesn't understand there is such a thing as a false conversion can be devastating. If we lack understanding that those who fail to repent are strangers to conversion, we're liable to think that simply praying a sinner's prayer or responding to an altar call gets someone saved.

2. Jesus told His disciples when they questioned Him about the Parable of the Sower, "Do you not understand this parable? How then will you understand all the parables?" (Mark 4:13). In other words, the Parable of the Sower is the key to unlocking the mysteries of all the other parables.

3. Six characteristics of a false convert in the Parable of the Sower:

    1. Immediate results (Mark 4:5)
    2. Lack of moisture (Luke 8:6)
    3. No root (Matt. 13:6)
    4. Receive the word with gladness (Mark 4:16)
    5. Receive the word with joy (Matt. 13:20)
    6. They do "believe" for a season (Luke 8:13)

4. James 2:19 says, "You believe that there is one God. You do well. Even the demons believe—and tremble!" This verse reveals that mere belief—when not accompanied by repentance (Luke 13:3) and placing one's faith in Christ (Acts 20:21)—is not sufficient for salvation.

5. Five fruits of a true convert:

    1. Fruit of repentance (Matt. 3:8)
    2. Fruit of thanksgiving (Heb. 13:15)

3. Fruit of good works (Col. 1:10)
4. Fruit of the Spirit (Gal. 5:22-23)
5. Fruit of righteousness (Phil. 1:11)

6. Tribulation, temptation, and persecution.

7. The false convert will be exposed as a hypocrite on Judgment Day, when the wheat and the tares will be separated.

8. The Wheat and Tares (true and false), the Good Fish and Bad Fish (true and false), the Foolish Virgins and the Wise Virgins (true and false), and the Sheep and Goats (true and false).

9. We can make sure we are not responsible for bringing false converts into the Church by making it paramount to preach biblically. That means using the Law to bring a knowledge of sin. It means mentioning Judgment Day, not casually, but impressing upon the mind of our hearer that he must face a holy God and answer for every sin he has committed against Him. It also means preaching the cross and the necessity of repentance. We should avoid modern methods where emotions are stirred in an effort to get decisions. We may rejoice over decisions, but heaven reserves its rejoicing for repentance.

BONUS answer:

Matthew 7:15: False prophets
Mark 13:22: False christs
2 Corinthians 11:13: False apostles
Galatians 2:4: False brethren
2 Peter 2:1: False teachers

SESSION 4

WHAT DID JESUS DO?

This video teaching goes live onto the streets of Southern California to show you how these principles pan out in actual use. We pray this video will inspire you to get out of your comfort zone and into the harvest field!

NOTES:

_____

_____

_____

_____

_____

_____

_____

_____

_____

_____

_____

_____

_____

_____

_____

_____

_____

_____

_____

Session 4 Quiz

Read this article, and then answer the questions that follow it.

Personal Witnessing–What Did Jesus Do?

To share our faith effectively, we must show people that we care by being friendly. Practice on people at the park, gas station, or grocery store, with a simple, "Hi, how are you?" or, "Good morning! Nice day, isn't it?" If the person responds warmly, we may then ask, "Do you live around here?" and develop a conversation.

In talking with the woman at the well, Jesus began in the natural realm (everyday things). You may want to do the same by talking about sports or the weather, then perhaps using something in the news to transition to spiritual things. Another simple way to swing to the spiritual is to offer a gospel tract and ask, "Did you get one of these?" When the person takes it, say, "It's a gospel tract. Do you have a Christian background?"

Then by following the WDJD outline, you can confidently lead any witnessing encounter. You'll know exactly where you are in a conversation and exactly where it is going. You can say good-bye to your fears! Let's follow the way of the Master given in Luke 18:18–21. Jesus first addressed the man's understanding of good.

W: Would you consider yourself to be a good person?

People are not offended by this question, because you are asking about their favorite subject—themselves. Expect them to respond, "Yes, I'm a pretty good person." This reveals their pride and self-righteousness. At this point you are ready to use the Law (the Ten Commandments) to humble them . . . the way Jesus did.

D: Do you think you have kept the Ten Commandments?

With the rich, young ruler, Jesus used the Law to bring "the knowledge of sin" (Rom. 3:20). We can do the same by asking this question. Most people think they have, so follow with, "Let's take a look at a few and see. Have you ever told a lie?" This may seem confrontational, but if asked in a spirit of love, there won't be any offense. Remember that the "work of the Law [is] written in their hearts" and their conscience will bear "witness" (Rom. 2:15). Have confidence that the conscience will do its work and affirm the truth of each Commandment.

Some will admit to lying; others will say they have told only "white lies." Ask, "What does that make you?" They will hesitate to say, but get them to admit, "A liar." Continue going through the Commandments. Ask, "Have you ever stolen something, even if it's small?" Ask, "What does that make you?" and press them to say, "A thief." Say, "Jesus said, 'Whoever looks at a woman to lust for her has already committed adultery with her in his heart.' Have you ever looked at someone with lust?"

Then ask, "Have you ever taken the Lord's name in vain?" Gently explain, "So instead of using a four-letter filth word to express disgust, you've taken the name of the One who gave you life and everything that is precious to you, and you have dragged it through the mud. That's called 'blasphemy,' and God promises that He will not hold anyone blameless who takes His name in vain."

At this point, the individual will either grow quiet (his "mouth may be stopped" by the Law, Rom. 3:19) or will be getting agitated. Ask his name and say, "John, by your own admission, you're a lying thief, a blasphemer, and an adulterer at heart, and we've only looked at four of the Ten Commandments."

J–Judgment: If God judges you by the Ten Commandments on the Day of Judgment, will you be innocent or guilty?

If he says he will be innocent, say, "You just told me that you broke God's Law. Think about it. Will you be innocent or guilty?" It's very important that you get an admission of guilt.

D–Destiny: Will you go to heaven or hell?

People won't be offended because you are simply asking a question, rather than telling them where they're going. From there the conversation may go one of three ways:

1. *He may confidently say, "I don't believe in hell."* Gently respond, "That doesn't matter. You still have to face God on Judgment Day whether you believe in it or not. If I step onto the freeway when a massive truck is heading for me and I say, 'I don't believe in trucks,' my lack of belief isn't going to change reality."

2. *He may admit he's guilty, but say he'll go to heaven.* He may think God is "good" and will therefore overlook sin in his case. Point out that if a judge has a guilty murderer standing before him, if he's a good judge, he can't just let him go. He must ensure that the guilty man is punished. If God is good, He must punish murderers, rapists, thieves, liars, adulterers, and those who live in rebellion to the inner light God has given every man. Tenderly tell him he has already admitted that he's lied, stolen, blasphemed, and committed adultery in

his heart, and that God gave him a conscience so he'd know right from wrong.

3. *He may admit that he is guilty and therefore going to hell.* Ask if that concerns him. Speak about how much he values his eyes and how much more therefore he should value the salvation of his soul.

To give him the good news, follow the outline CCRAFT: Concern, Cross, Repentance And Faith, Truth. If the person has been humbled and admits he's concerned, then you have the privilege of sharing the cross with him, encouraging him to repent and place his faith in the Savior. If he's willing to confess and forsake his sins, have him pray and ask God to forgive him. Then pray for him. Point him to the truth of the Bible, instructing him to read it daily and obey what he reads, and get into a Bible-believing church.

1.   How should you begin talking with an unbeliever?

   _____
   _____
   _____
   _____
   _____

2.   Give two possible ways you could swing the conversation to the spiritual.

   _____
   _____
   _____
   _____

3. Tell how you would bring conviction using the Law.

    _____
    _____
    _____
    _____

4. How should you give the good news to a sinner?

    _____
    _____
    _____
    _____

For the answers to this quiz, simply review the article.

ENDNOTES

Chapter 1: What Peter Feared

1. John Newton, "Faith—Spiritual Knowledge—Seeking—True Repentance," Letter to the Reverend Mr. S—, December 8, 1775.

Chapter 2: Irksome Words That Convict

1. Ray Comfort, *The Evidence Bible* (Gainesville, FL: Bridge-Logos Publishers, 2003).
2. J. C. Ryle, cited by C.H. Spurgeon, *Spurgeon's Sermon Notes,* (Grand Rapids, MI: Kregel Publications 1990), p. 277.
3. Charles Haddon Spurgeon, *Spurgeon at His Best,* compiled by Tom Carter (Grand Rapids, MI: Baker Book House, 1991), p. 67.
4. Bill Bright, "A Personal Word from Dr. Bill Bright," *10 Basic Steps to Christian Maturity*. http://www.tenbasicsteps.org/english/personalword.htm (accessed March 2009).
5. David Colins, *God's Leader For a Nation: Abraham Lincoln* (Fenton, MI: Mott Media, 1976), p. 144.
6. According to The Barna Group, "there are approximately 101 million born-again Christians." http://www.barna.org/FlexPage.aspx?Page=Topic&TopicID=8 (2006 data).
7. Another resource that I often use in evangelism is a million-dollar tract. The front of the bill resembles a unit of currency, and the gospel message is written on the back of the bill. More than 20 million of these tracts have been sold (available at www.livingwaters.com). They are extremely popular, because they are so easy to give away. They have a *perceived* value.

Chapter 5: For Heaven's Applause

1. You can read the whole story in *Out of the Comfort Zone* (Gainesville, FL: Bridge-Logos Publishers, 2004).

Chapter 6: The Question of Eternal Destiny

1. Charles Haddon Spurgeon, *Morning and Evening* (Wheaton, IL: Good News Publishers, 2003), February 19.

Chapter 8: They Need to Hear the Moral Law

1. Manu Raju, "National Debt Hits Record $11 Trillion," Politico, March 17, 2009. http://www.politico.com/news/stories/0309/20139.html (accessed April 2009).
2. "How Common Is Cancer?" Aetna InteliHealth. http://www.intelihealth.com/IH/ihtIH/WSIHW000/8096/24516/362246.html?d=dmtContent (accessed April 2009).
3. "United States Crime Rates 1960-2007," The Disaster Center, data based on FBI Uniform Crime Reports. http://www.disastercenter.com/crime/uscrime.htm (accessed April 2009).
4. "Abortion Statistics in the United States: Statistics and Trends," National Right to Life, 2007 data. http://www.nrlc.org/ABORTION/facts/abortionstats.html (accessed April 2009).
5. "Cyber-sex: The New Affair Treatment Considerations," *Journal of Couple and Relationship Therapy,* vol. 1, no. 3, pp. 37-56.
6. Jonathan Turley, "Of Lust and the Law," *The Washington Post,* September 5, 2004. http://www.washingtonpost.com/wp-dyn/articles/A62581-2004Sep4.html (accessed April 2009).

7. "Births: Preliminary Data for 2007," National Vital Statistics Reports, vol. 57, no. 12, March 18, 2009. http://www.cdc.gov/nchs/data/nvsr/nvsr57/nvsr57_12.pdf+%22National +Center+for+Health+Statistics%22+one-third+of+births&cd=1&hl=en&ct=clnk&gl= us&client=firefox-a (accessed April 2009).
8. Lawrence K. Altman, "Sex Infections Found in Quarter of Teenage Girls," *The New York Times,* March 12, 2008. http://www.nytimes.com/2008/03/12/science/12std.html?_r=1 (accessed April 2009).
9. Dan Ackman, "How Big Is Porn?" *Forbes,* May 25, 2001. http://www.forbes.com/2001/ 05/25/0524porn.html (accessed April 2009).
10. N.C. Aizenman, "New High in U.S. Prison Numbers," *The Washington Post,* February 29, 2008. http://www.washingtonpost.com/wp-dyn/content/story/2008/02/28/ST2008022803016. html (accessed April 2009).
11. James Patterson and Peter Kim, *The Day America Told the Truth* (New York: Prentice Hall, 1991).

Chapter 9: The "Fine" Has Been Paid!
1. Matthew Henry, *Matthew Henry's Commentary on the Whole Bible* (Peabody, MA: Hendrickson Publishers, 1991), Romans 7:7-14a.
2. Congressman Xavier Becerra, "National Crime Gun Identification Act," February 7, 2008. http://becerra.house.gov/HoR/CA31/Issues/Microstamping+Page.htm (accessed April 2009).
3. Don't try this at home. The curved screens on computers and TVs are almost unbreakable. On the movie set, I smashed a wooden bat and then broke a steal bat in half when trying to break the screen. We had to drill holes in the glass before it would break on screen.
4. Portions of this section are adapted from *Revival's Golden Key* (Gainesville, FL: Bridge-Logos, 2002). Used by permission.
5. The Barna Group, 2007 study. http://www.barna.org/FlexPage.aspx?Page=Topic&TopicID=8.
6. C. H. Spurgeon, "The Perpetuity of the Law of God," sermon delivered on May 21, 1882.

Chapter 10: The Quicksand of Moral Relativity
1. Portions of this chapter have been adapted from *The Charles Darwin Bible* by Ray Comfort (Nashville, TN: Holman Bible Outreach International, 2009).
2. Bill O'Reilly, "Reaching Critical Mass," July 11, 2002, WorldNetDaily. http://www.worldnet daily.com/index.php?pageId=14523 (accessed April 2009).

Chapter 11: It May Take Time
1 The Law is used so often in Scripture as an evangelistic tool that I wrote an entire book on the subject, *What Did Jesus Do?* (Gainesville, FL: Bridge-Logos Publishers, 2005).
2. I often use the phrase, "You broke God's Law, and Jesus paid your fine."
3. C.H. Spurgeon, "Law and Grace," sermon delivered August 26, 1855.
4. "The Ethics of American Youth—2008 Summary," Josephson Institute Center for Youth Ethics, December 2008 study. http://charactercounts.org/programs/reportcard/ (accessed March 2009).
5. The Barna Group, 1994 study. http://www.barna.org/FlexPage.aspx?Page=Topic&TopicID=8.
6. "Abortion Facts," The Center for Bio-Ethical Reform, data © 1997, The Alan Guttmacher Institute (www.agi-usa.org) and © 1995, 1998 *Family Planning Perspectives.* http://www.abor tionno.org/Resources/fastfacts.html (accessed May 2009).

7. See *The Way of the Master* (Gainesville, FL: Bridge-Logos Publishers, 2006) for statistics.
8. C.H. Spurgeon, "Apostolic Exhortation," sermon on Acts 3:19 delivered April 5, 1868.
9. "The Four Spiritual Laws," Wikipedia.com, November 12, 2008. http://en.wikipedia.org/wiki/The_Four_Spiritual_Laws (accessed April 2009).
10. "Campus Crusade History," Campus Crusade for Christ, 2008. http://www.campuscrusadeforchrist.com/aboutus/history.htm (accessed April 2009).
11. Bill Bright, *Heaven or Hell: Your Ultimate Choice* (Peachtree City, GA: New Life Publications, 2002), pp. 32, 48.

Chapter 13: Speaking to Intellectuals

1. Parts of this chapter have been adapted from *The Atheist Bible* (Nashville, TN: B&H, 2009).
2. "Do We Live Again?" Interview with Thomas Edison as quoted in *The Illustrated London News,* May 3, 1924. See http://atheisme.free.fr/Quotes/Edison.htm (accessed March 2009).
3. *The Atlantic Monthly,* vol. 128, no. 4 (October 1921), p. 520, as quoted in Francis Trevelyan Miller, *Thomas A. Edison, Benefactor of Mankind: The Romantic Life Story of the World's Greatest Inventor* (Philadelphia: John C. Winston Co., 1931), p. 293.
4. Henry Ford, as quoted in Miller, *Thomas A. Edison, Benefactor of Mankind: The Romantic Life Story of the World's Greatest Inventor,* p. 294.
5. Mark Twain, "The American Vandal," speech given in 1868-1869. http://etext.virginia.edu/railton/innocent/vandtext.html (accessed March 2009).
6. Connie Ann Kirk, *Mark Twain: A Biography* (Westport, CT: Greenwood Press, 2004).
7. Albert Bigelow Paine, *Mark Twain's Notebook,* 1902-1903 (New York: Harper & Row, 1935).
8. Gary Sloan, "Robert Frost: Old Testament Christian or Atheist?" January 28, 2003. http://www.liberator.net/articles/SloanGary/RobertFrost.html (accessed March 2009).
9. Susan B. Anthony, "Sentencing in the Case of *United States vs. Susan B. Anthony* on the Charge of Illegal Voting," June 17-18, 1873. http://www.law.umkc.edu/faculty/projects/ftrials/anthony/sentencing.html (accessed March 2009).
10. Susan B. Anthony, quoted in Ida Husted Harper, *The Life and Work of Susan B. Anthony,* (Indianapolis, IN: Bowen-Merrill, 1898), p. 853.
11. Susan B. Anthony, "Constitutional Argument: Speech After Being Convicted of Voting in the 1872 Presidential Election," Monroe County, New York, 1872-1873. http://gos.sbc.edu/a/anthony.html (accessed March 2009).
12. Ibid.
13. "Student Essay on Love as a Religion in *A Farewell to Arms.*" http://www.bookrags.com/essay-2005/11/25/14119/869 (accessed March 2009).
14. "Earnest Hemingway Biography." http://www.biographybase.com/biography/Hemingway_Ernest.html (accessed March 2009).
15. Albert Einstein, according to the testimony of Prince Hubertus of Lowenstein, as quoted in Ronald W. Clark, *Einstein: The Life and Times* (New York: World Publishing Company, 1971), p. 425. http://www.stephenjaygould.org/ctrl/quotes_einstein.html (accessed March 2009).
16. Interview in *The Jewish Sentinel,* September 1931, quoted in Fred R. Shapiro, *The Yale Book of Quotations* (New Haven, CT: Yale University Press, 2006), p. 229.
17. Alice Calaprice, ed., *The Expanded Quotable Einstein* (Princeton: Princeton University Press, 2000), pp. 202-218.
18. "What Life Means to Einstein," Interview with G. Viereck, *Saturday Evening Post,* October 26, 1929.
19. Einstein to an unidentified addressee, August 7, 1941 (Einstein Archive, reel 54-927).

20. Quoted in an interview in *The Saturday Evening Post*, 1929.
21. Ibid.
22. Abraham Pais, *Subtle Is the Lord: The Science and the Life of Albert Einstein* (New York: Oxford University Press, 1982), p. 319.

Chapter 16: True Conversion
1. C.H. Spurgeon, *The Metropolitan Tabernacle Pulpit: Sermons by Charles Haddon Spurgeon* (London: Passmore & Alabaster, 1875), pp. 208-209.
2. You can listen to these messages online at www.livingwaters.com.
3. C.H. Spurgeon, "A Sermon" (No. 1889), Delivered February 28, 1886 at the Metropolitan Tabernacle, Newington.

Chapter 17: The Fruit of Biblical Evangelism
1. See www.ambassadorsalliance.com.
2. Emeal "EZ" Zwayne, Tony "Lawman" Miano, Stuart "Scotty" Scott and Mark Spence (the Dean of the School of Biblical Evangelism).
3. The sequence is in season 2 of *The Way of the Master*.
4. It was also aired on ABC's *Nightline*, May 9, 2007.
5. See Ray Comfort and Kirk Cameron, *The Way of the Master* (Gainesville, FL: Bridge-Logos Publishers, 2006) for statistics showing that 80 to 90 percent of decisions obtained by local churches and large crusades fall away from the faith.

FREE ONLINE RESOURCES

Visit www.WayOfTheMaster.com to discover some of the many free resources that are available to help you reach the lost with the gospel:

- Sign-up to receive our free weekly update. Exciting things are continually happening with our ministry, and if you are not signed up, you will never know.
- Listen to numerous audio and video teachings.
- Sample three actual lessons from our online School of Biblical Evangelism.
- Check out more than 200 common questions, objections and other commentary from *The Evidence Bible*.
- Explore the many other free articles and tools to encourage and equip you to better share your faith.
- Check out the comprehensive DVD study *The Basic Training Course* for further grounding in these principles.

Here is what some have said about *The Way of the Master*, our foundational book on evangelism:

"Dynamic. . . compelling." —Dr. D. James Kennedy

"A powerful light in the darkness of our times." —Dr. Jerry Falwell

"A shattering publication!" —Leonard Ravenhill

"I have over one thousand books on evangelism, soul-winning and revival in my personal library and none of them are worthy to be compared to this book." —R. W. Jones

"*The Way of the Master*, in my opinion, is the best book ever written on evangelism." —Ron Begin

ALSO AVAILABLE FROM
KIRK CAMERON &
RAY COMFORT

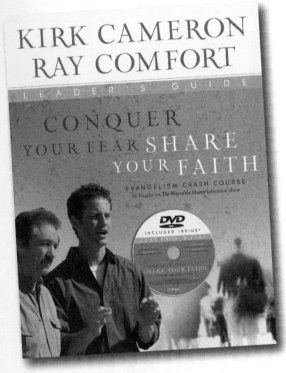

**CONQUER YOUR FEAR,
SHARE YOUR FAITH
LEADER'S GUIDE**
Kirk Cameron and Ray Comfort
ISBN 978.08307.51525
ISBN 08307.51521

Evangelism is like swimming. You can talk about it until you are blue in the face, but if you don't dive in and do it, you will never swim. This course is all about diving in. Ray Comfort and Kirk Cameron, the cohosts of *The Way of the Master* TV series and radio program, have put together this simple and flexible curriculum for those in churches or small groups who want to obey the Bible's command to tell others about Jesus. In four complete lessons (which can be presented in a one-day "crash" course or in four separate weekly sessions), Kirk and Ray will guide participants step by step through their straightforward approach to evangelism. Those who complete the course will have every tool they need to overcome their fear and talk about their faith with friends, neighbors, coworkers and even strangers! Includes course schedules, student handouts and materials, and accompanying DVD.